# THE CONRAN HOME DECORATOR
# STORAGE SOLUTIONS

# THE CONRAN HOME DECORATOR
# STORAGE SOLUTIONS

GILLY LOVE

VILLARD BOOKS
NEW YORK 1986

Please note. The photographs have been collected
from all over the world to show as varied a range
of ideas as possible within the scope of this
book, so that not all the items featured are
available through Conran's.

Conceived, designed and produced by
Conran Octopus Limited
28-32 Shelton Street
London WC2 9PH

Project editor: Liz Wilhide
Art editor: Jane Willis
Editor: Judy Martin
Designer: Dave Allen
Picture research: Keith Bernstein

Library of Congress Catalog Card Number: 85-45449
ISBN: 0-394-74400-4

Printed and bound in Hong Kong
9 8 7 6 5 4 3 2
First American Edition

# CONTENTS

# STORAGE WITH STYLE

Careful planning is needed if storage provision is to match both the style of your home and your budget. It takes time to evolve an individual and distinctive style, and your home should complement and reflect your own interests and way of life. Its appearance makes a statement about how you choose the things you live with and assemble the different elements – color, lighting, furnishings.

Finding the happy balance between personal taste and practical function also means juggling with available funds. Financial constraints often lead to better solutions. Limited resources force you to stop and assess each purchase or decorating decision.

Don't be deceived by those interiors that look thrown together but work as if by magic: it is likely that more thought has gone into them than you would ever imagine. Before deciding on a furnishing and decorative scheme, work out as clearly as possible how each room relates to the next and how they are individually used. Storage must be part of these initial plans as it may affect the colors, shapes and patterns you choose or the types of lighting you select. Be practical and alert to the combination of function and attractive design. Display shelves that include stereo housing need electrical outlets close by or built into the wall itself; the effect of a subtle wallpaper may be spoiled by the presence of a large imposing wardrobe, but a built-in cupboard with doors decorated in the same paper can look perfectly sympathetic.

Build into your plans a degree of flexibility too; a small pile of books quickly grows into a sizeable library and several pieces of delicate china could easily develop into a collecting habit. Know yourself; if you're naturally untidy, don't think that stringent storage will change the habits of a lifetime. Chaotically packed shelves that can be instantly concealed with blinds and a vast wardrobe where clothes are simply hooked or hung rather than carefully folded are good storage solutions that don't make extra work.

Providing well-designed storage has to be an integral part of the initial planning of all interior spaces and, in today's smaller homes, it's essential to make the most of every inch of available space. Clever use of color and light has helped to make the most of this tiny sleeping area, but it is the carefully designed and well-organized storage that actually makes the whole scheme work. This room has been divided into two areas, one providing a generous, open space for dining and entertaining visitors. The other end has been meticulously planned to integrate a sleeping platform with desk space, a library in the alcove above the bed, with a wardrobe space concealed by drapes on the right of the platform. Further clothes' storage is provided by generous-sized drawers under the platform at the foot of the bed. Two mini chests of drawers make perfectly proportioned jewellery boxes and side-tables for the desk lamp which doubles up as a bedside reading light. Cane blinds adjusted by a simple pulley can be lowered to conceal the whole or just part of this arrangement.

# DISPLAY AND CONCEALMENT

Some possessions we like to show off, while others are best hidden away. These two categories can loosely be applied to all storage requirements, and suitable fittings devised to deal with either case. Masterpieces of storage furniture make display objects in their own right, whereas other solutions, such as wall-to-wall wardrobes, are often better concealed behind mirrored or wallpapered doors. Certain functional objects are more efficiently used when easily seen and readily accessible. If you tend to be lazy about putting things away, you might as well keep them on view in their proper place, rather than add to their inelegance by letting them accumulate in an inappropriate setting. On the other hand, shallow cupboards and drawers that open smoothly can conveniently hide a multitude of sins.

**Showing off**

Display objects can be further sub-divided into functional and non-functional. Ornaments may be considered as non-functional – except that they provide immense visual pleasure. They are often the decorative details which give a home its distinctive identity and style. Possessions are very individual, and what may be junk and clutter to some are objects of beauty and sentimentality to others. A handful of shells carefully collected and arranged on glass shelves costs next to nothing but looks stunning, recalling happy memories of summer holidays. Whatever you prize deserves showing off, whether priceless china or matchbox toys, and it may take time to find the best way of making the most of it.

Family heirlooms of antique porcelain are safest behind glass doors, where they'll be seen but need only occasional dusting; smaller collections, such as thimbles or miniature toys, fit neatly into the sections of an old printing tray, hung on the wall to make a colorful montage. With a little ingenuity you can make a display that has a dual function. An open case on low legs and fitted with a glass lid can be used as an occasional table; the objects beneath the glass are clearly seen but safely under cover. A large terra-cotta pot covered with a finished glass top conceals an uplighter inside; this will bring a soft glow to an alcove or dim corner of the room, while

*Left: Open cubes make one of the most versatile modern storage solutions, with limitless possibilities. In this case they provide the focal point usually created by a fireplace.*

*Below: Open shelving across a room-divide utilizes space without blocking any light or view. Kitchen objects lend themselves particularly well to open storage.*

highlighting your prettiest ornaments set out on top of the glass. A mantelpiece is a prime spot for treasures, but don't be afraid to leave space for the sake of space, so that individual pieces can be clearly appreciated. Consider how these objects may be best lit; sometimes the shadows they create are as interesting as the items themselves. Move things around; exchange some for different pieces now and again. Without any expenditure on redecorating, a room can be

*Left: Wardrobes need not be a solid wall of doors: mirrors add lively interest, reflecting the light from the windows opposite.*
*Right: A bedroom basin is simply concealed with blinds.*

made to look fresh and interesting merely by adding and subtracting some of the things we already own.

Many functional objects require display to be clearly seen and within easy reach. Record albums stacked at eye level are more often played than those partly concealed on dark shelves near the floor. An oven glove hooked up next to the cooker is easier to grab when a saucepan is seconds away from boiling over. Useful items cease to be so if they're difficult to get at; an electric juicer stored at the back of a cupboard is quickly forgotten if there is no convenient socket and a plastic lemon-squeezer happens to be close to hand.

## Covering up

Items we deliberately conceal are for the most part better kept that way. Fine homemade preserves make delicious displays, but when kept in a cool, dark cupboard their shelf-life is considerably lengthened. Clothes are displayed when we wear them and their peak condition is maintained if they are otherwise stored carefully inside a dust-free wardrobe. Out of sight should not mean out of mind and concealment needs as much thought as display. It's usually the little things that find a loophole in the organization – needles, fuse wire, light bulbs – things you can do without for months and then suddenly need right away. Wherever you hide such things, work out the places that you can logically find, however unconventional they may appear to others.

Don't feel obliged to conceal things because of bulky or unattractive packaging. If the washing powder box is too big for the store cupboard, decant the contents into something you can display, a bread box or large stoneware pot. Shelving can store multitudes of useful but unattractive objects. The crowded shelves can be neatly hidden by roller blinds, but practically revealed in seconds. Large, unwieldy appliances should be given their own place: the vacuum cleaner and, worse still, the ironing board take up too much space in a kitchen; they are short on visual appeal and are better concealed under the stairs, in a shallow closet or in the spare room. It is always a good idea to consider where to store things when you buy them.

Large cupboards are prime targets for hiding things away in a disorganized jumble to make the rest of the room appear tidy. Not only are the contents often forgotten and assumed lost, but much of the storage space itself is wasted. Cardboard boxes from supermarkets cost nothing; filled with all manner of things, they effectively double the size of the same space when stacked vertically. If you label each box as you fill it, it saves rooting through all the wrong ones when you go searching for a specific item.

# MODULAR AND SPECIFIC STORAGE

Modular and specific furniture are in many ways at opposite ends of the storage spectrum. Your choice to some extent depends on whether you prefer the appearance of purpose-built furniture which proclaims its specific function, or more anonymous, streamlined units used to conceal or display the items stored in them. Other important factors are the amount of space available and the immediacy of particular storage requirements.

### Modular storage
Modular storage offers you the convenience of adding units as and when finances or space permit; many systems can also be easily rearranged and moved from room to room. One of the best and most flexible is the cube system. Based on a simple wooden or plastic box, open or shelved, contents may be freely displayed or concealed by the addition of extra details such as deep or shallow drawers or cupboard fronts. This system offers many possible configurations: two units side by side as a bedside chest; one on top of another as a plant stand; four in a square as a low living room table; eight stacked together as a tall bookcase. Other designs offer a wider selection of basic units, including cabinets with transparent or opaque doors, often with adjustable shelves, and flap-down tops on open cases and drawer units. With complete systems like these you can create library storage or display cabinets.

In the better quality furniture of this kind, the units are well finished at the backs, so storage pieces can be placed at right-angles to the wall or as freestanding room dividers. A system arranged in this way may improve the dimensions of a large room, giving greater flexibility and saving wall space for other purposes. Cheaper modular furniture may be dramatically improved by a couple of coats of paint or by changing door and drawer handles for ones of superior quality.

### Furniture for a specific purpose
Modular storage systems have evolved over the past few decades to meet the changing and growing needs of modern living. Old storage furniture tends to fall into specific cate-

Modular storage is flexible, can be built up over a period of time, and is useful for filling awkward corners without the expense of building in. Most systems combine open and closed units so that jumble can be hidden and prettier objects displayed. A combination of function and decoration is a more attractive way to use space than either alone.

## Modular shelving

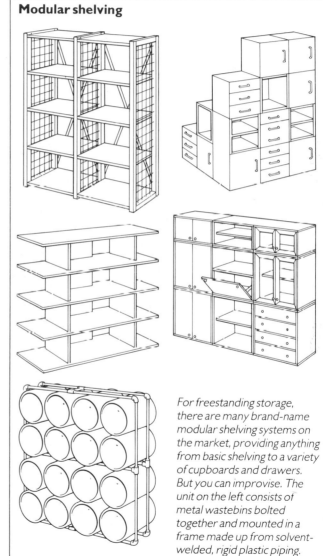

For freestanding storage, there are many brand-name modular shelving systems on the market, providing anything from basic shelving to a variety of cupboards and drawers. But you can improvise. The unit on the left consists of metal wastebins bolted together and mounted in a frame made up from solvent-welded, rigid plastic piping.

*Left: The fine craftsmanship and strong character of old furniture can often be adapted to suit modern needs without drastically changing the original design or function. In this Victorian-style bathroom, an old-fashioned washstand has been brought up to date by plumbing in taps and setting a basin into the marble top. Though drawer space is lost, the washstand still provides storage in the generous cupboard beneath the sink.*

*Above: This chest was probably part of the furnishings of an old grocer's or chemist's shop and its numerous drawers of all shapes and sizes make an ideal place to store dress-making equipment.*

*Clothes, otherwise draped across a bedroom, are simply hung from this wigwam of sticks: a practical addition to guest rooms or for taking the bulge from a crammed wardrobe.*

gories, from a time when natural materials like wood were more plentiful and therefore cheaper, and when homes were filled with much more furniture than is the preference today. Late nineteenth-century fashion, for example, adored dark mahogany pieces cluttering up the rooms – which was all well and good in generously proportioned homes with live-in housekeepers to keep them well polished. Much of this old furniture is massive, but solid and beautifully made, and individual pieces can work just as well in contemporary settings. The popularity of the appearance and fine crafts-manship of old furniture has increasingly led to new designs built on old models and contemporary pieces are available that have the same sense of solidity combined with elegance.

Besides providing an interesting focal point to a room, much of this furniture may be used for purposes other than those for which it was specifically designed. It's worth remembering that outdated furniture can often be turned to a new use if you put your mind to it. For instance, in a dining or living room a mahogany linen press can make an elegant bar with drawers used to store table linen and silver. A small pine dresser may be just the thing for a child's room, displaying treasured objects and toys on the shelves, with clothes stored in the cupboards or drawers beneath. A pedestal desk with a mass of tiny drawers turns into a perfect dressing table with storage of just the right size for cosmetics, perfumes and jewelery.

Contemporary designs for specific types of furniture tend to feature largely in the kitchen, where practicality usually dictates a function for every inch of space. Wire grocery drawers, carousel shelves for corner cupboards and tiered vegetable trolleys are adaptable as ideal modular systems for clothes, cosmetics and toys, and for storage in the home office. Furniture designed specifically for one type of storage is in fact often multi-functional, bearing in mind what best suits your needs, taste and budget. An all-purpose tubular steel trolley may not be so desirable, or so mobile, in a home with thick rugs on bare floors or in a room furnished throughout with antiques.

# BUILT-IN AND FREE-STANDING FURNITURE

When making a choice between built-in and freestanding storage, you need to consider the appearance you would like it to have and balance this with the style and structural characteristics of the interior architecture. There is also the important choice between permanence and mobility. Whichever you choose, the storage system should add visual interest to a room as well as performing a function for you. It need not be obtrusive or seem to crowd in on the living space. One wall of a living room filled with custom-built shelves may provide all the storage you need, make an interesting focal point and free the rest of the room from clutter, thus creating an illusion of more space than is actually there.

In older homes, with alcoves either side of the chimney breast, irregular walls, protruding bare boards and picture rails, building-in is a possible solution but the quirks and individuality of each room deserve consideration too. Built-in means the furniture is there to stay and should look as though it has always been there. This means continuing cornices, picture rails and bare boards around floor-to-ceiling storage. Hardwood moldings glued to plywood doors and shelf edges before painting often supply new furniture with a style in keeping with other structural details.

Radiators are not an original feature of most homes and, though essential, may be far from attractive. They can be disguised by storage units built above and around them. Once painted to match the walls, both storage and radiator blend into the background.

A modern house or apartment with box dimensions may cry out for some architectural definition. Simple alcoves filled with shelves fitted between plasterboard partitions can improve the room's original proportions. A permanent partition can divide one room into two more interesting spaces, with storage combining a variety of functions on either side — a bar above a wine cupboard, a desk in a bookshelf unit. Tailor your storage to the possessions you have and those you are likely to accumulate. Customized storage designed for a music library must have flexibility; you are hardly likely to stop collecting records just because all the

*Left: Built-in furniture needs to take into account the architectural style of a room. The numerous partitions of this library follow similar lines in the room's casement windows.*

*Below: This awkward gap has wisely been chosen to conceal a radiator behind a rattan panel. Two simple shelves above it make no attempt to fill the remaining space.*

shelves originally built have been filled.

It is difficult to visualize permanent storage and you could try experimenting with a freestanding item of similar dimensions borrowed from another room. Study neighboring homes to see how others have solved storage problems, but bring a critical eye to bear and learn by their mistakes.

Traditional, reproduction and antique furniture, usually acquired for appearance rather than function, should still work to enhance and complement a room. It may take a long time to find a piece that is exactly right. Keep the measurements of a particular recess or specific wall with you wherever you go. An expensive antique may not be such a wise investment if it does not fit where you intended it should – it may not even be persuaded to go through your front door.

## Self-assembly units

Most of today's freestanding storage is designed and made for quick assembly. Self-assembly, knock-down or flat-pack are all terms used by manufacturers to describe the type of furniture you put together yourself at home. On the whole such units tend to be cheaper, but only because, packed flat, they take up less space in shops and warehouses and need fewer staff to handle them. Less expensive does not necessarily mean less good. Also, it is far easier to take home a large shelving system in kit form than to negotiate tight corners and narrow staircases with a pre-assembled unit. As an added bonus, of course, even sturdy and quite complex items can be dismantled and reerected if you move house.

Self-assembly open shelving units, particularly those with adjustable shelves, are practical for displaying a whole range of different items and make simple but very functional room dividers, with easy access from both sides. More flexible storage is achieved with those systems which consist of different individual units – open shelves, cupboards with glass or wood doors and drawers. They can be combined as you like, added to or rearranged if your life-style alters, you move or you simply feel like a change. These systems have so many permutations they can easily be adapted to meet any new situation.

## Self-assembly furniture

### DON'T

- order furniture by mail order if there is no opportunity to see before you buy. Glossy advertisements and catalogues often disguise inferior quality; photographs can give a distorted view of size and proportions.

- take away a self-assembly pack from a showroom or warehouse without checking that all the components, including a full set of instructions, are there.

- deal with a large item of furniture single-handed. You might damage yourself or the unit, and two heads are better than one for deciphering cryptic instructions.

- tighten screws fully until the whole assembly is complete unless instructions state otherwise.

- be tempted to modify the construction until you have put it together as instructed to see how the design works.

### DO

- examine a fully assembled sample before you buy. Check that the dimensions will fit the intended space and look at the small print for details such as adjustable shelving.

- unpack the components carefully and keep them together near the place where the assembled unit will stand. Put them on a soft rug or blanket if the floor is not carpeted.

- read all instructions carefully before you get to work. Run them through in your mind and if they are unclear contact the manufacturer or supplier for further advice.

- make sure you have the right tools to hand; usually a screwdriver is all that is necessary and specific items such as keys or wrenches may be supplied with the kit.

- lift the assembled furniture into place without pulling or dragging to avoid stresses that may loosen fixings or damage parts.

- go back to the store and complain if you are dissatisfied with the result or some of the components are damaged.

Below: This storage system and room divider is assembled exactly where it is to be used.

Bottom: Entire self-assembly kitchens are also available but need special care when fitting.

Below: Mobile storage relieves the congestion of overcrowded kitchen work surfaces.

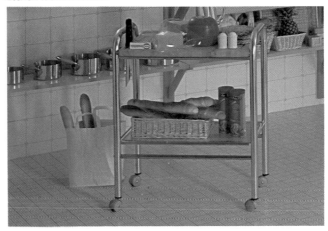

## Movable storage

Furniture that is even more flexible than freestanding units is the type of storage actually designed to be moved. The simple trolley is the solution for a vast range of items suitably kept on wheels. For example, hi-fi, television and video are bulky, heavy items, often needing a change of position for better sound and vision. They are more safely moved on wheeled bases.

Drinks and food trolleys move from the dining room to kitchen, kitchen to living room. They make useful serving tops and mobile side-tables, as well as providing a convenient method of clearing away. You can keep bottles and glasses or heavy serving dishes permanently stored on a trolley when they are out of use. In the kitchen, you can use a mobile work table with built-in chopping boards and knife racks, but check that wheels can be locked when necessary or the constant mobility will be an extreme disadvantage.

Vegetables are kept well ventilated in wire grid racks on castors, can be neatly stored under worktops, moved out for restocking and brought close to the sink for cleaning. These handy mobile baskets provide ingenious solutions for storage anywhere in the home. The best systems are those found at catering equipment and store fixture suppliers.

# ASSESSING YOUR NEEDS

Successful storage must be carefully planned and designed to suit you, your life-style, your home and possessions. The way you live is a reflection of your personality and, whether you're starting a home from scratch, updating an existing one or adding an extension, storage will be part of your plans. Good interior designers don't start a project until sure of their client's needs and requirements. Style is, of course, purely personal, the budget can be a restraint, comfort and practicality are highly important qualities – a well-designed home balances all these factors.

How we utilize space in our homes largely dictates how much we enjoy living in them. With more time to spend on leisure and creative activities, we need space to pursue them or they're quickly given up. Rooms today need to be multi-functional to make best use of restricted space; a bedroom can also be a playroom, sewing center, home office or quiet retreat for reading or listening to music. Endless resources don't necessarily result in perfectly planned homes; often severe budget limitations produce ingenious solutions that give more satisfaction than spending vast sums of money.

It makes sense first to decide the sort of person you are, taking your entire life-style into account, and then to design your home – and in this case the storage – to suit you. Some people seem to be naturally tidy, with homes where every-thing has a place – and stays there! Others are chronically messy. Some restrict their belongings to the bare minimum. Others are squirrels, people who keep everything – jam jars, newspapers, outgrown clothes and every theater program. These are extremes, of course, but whatever your person-ality, accepting it can help you find the kind of storage that will best work for you.

Sometimes a good clearout is all that's needed to make additional space. The annual spring cleaning used to provide an ideal opportunity, but that has rather faded into the past now that we have easy-clean surfaces, more efficient vacuum cleaners and dirt-free heating systems. The only time we tend to discard unwanted things and reorganize our homes completely is when we change house. Even an imaginary move can release all sorts of new space for storage. A door rehung to open in the opposite direction may give you an additional wall area for shelving or a cupboard. An entire room can be turned into a walk-in closet, freeing others altogether from providing space for storage. A small storage room turned into a generous wardrobe could free the space for a shower cubicle and wash basin in the bedroom, easing the burden on a tiny bathroom.

## Planning and reorganization

A good start is to take each room in turn, listing the items intended to be kept there. Divide the final list into items that deserve display rather than concealment, things that require easy, quick access, those for occasional use only. Check the storage you already have and consider ways of utilizing it more efficiently or moving it around between different rooms, before resorting to investment in new furniture.

If you do go shopping for new storage, take the exact dimensions of the whole room and the space where you intend to place a new item. Before you reach a final decision, there are various other considerations to be borne in mind.

Make sure you really like the furniture for itself and not just because it serves a particular function. If you don't care for it at the start, there's a good chance you'll grow to hate it in time. There is a parallel here with someone who buys an item of clothing several sizes too small as an incentive to lose weight, fails to do so and the garment becomes an object of loathing, an expensive mistake. It's better to wait until you've found something that matches your requirements exactly, in appearance, scale and function, and that may mean spending more than you intended. Some storage systems are designed to be bought in sections, added to when budgets permit. If you are considering this type of storage, check you are buying a well-established design from a reputable outlet, to ensure the range will still be available when you can afford new pieces. Check the versatility of these systems: how adjustable are the shelves, is there a choice between drawers or cupboard fronts, does the system need a wall to support it? If so, does it take into account base boards and picture rails, if you have them?

*Personal style controls choice of storage. Deep cupboards (left) conceal clutter, but here recessed shelves provide a visual break. For orderly types, open shelves (below) keep everything to hand.*

Compare prices; look at the cost difference between, say, a freestanding bookcase and one you can build in yourself or commission from a local carpenter. A library system, when full of books, may look very much the same as well-planned track shelving, but at twice the cost. Conversely, an unfinished wood system may cost the same as one with a teak veneer, but you can paint or stain it more easily.

Time spent on selecting the right storage to meet your budget and suit your home pays off as a good long-term investment. Fine quality and reasonably priced antiques are still to be found at auctions, particularly in out-of-town areas where there is less demand. Original designs produced as one-off pieces by up-and-coming designers, good modern classics and sympathetically made reproductions are likely to increase in value.

Well-designed, built-in storage can also add value to your property when you come to sell. Before you spend large amounts on custom-built furniture it is worth first considering how long you intend to live in your present home and the average annual increase of similar homes in the area. A fitted kitchen, for example, may help to sell your house but will not necessarily increase its value. As a rule of thumb, 10 per cent of the resale value is a guideline for how much to invest. Many inexpensive fitted kitchens can be vastly improved by the addition of a few interior details from a more expensive range that manufacturers offer as standard to their units, but which may also be bought separately. Ingenious hardware – 180-degree hinges, flap supports and self-locking stays – can also be used to customize large storage items such as wardrobes and desks.

# AREA BY AREA

One of the most important aspects of home interior design is the use of space. Unfortunately, not all rooms are the size and shape we'd like them to be. Clever use of color and light can help to create the illusion of space, but in reality it is well-planned and organized storage that actually makes space for space – and this has to be the ultimate luxury in most of today's smaller homes. How we utilize different areas of our homes largely dictates how much we enjoy living in them. Smaller homes demand less furniture, which in turn has to be more versatile and practical.

Modern storage furniture has to fulfill more than one function and be flexible enough to be used in several rooms. Beds with integral drawers, low chests that form coffee tables, seating that disguises cupboards or shelving: all these are practical ways of overcoming space restrictions. Apart from the furniture, the living spaces need to be made multi-functional, too. A dining room can double up as an extra bedroom or playroom, a storage room can be halved and made to serve as a tiny home office and a walk-in wardrobe. The important criterion is to make your space adaptable to the needs of its regular occupants.

The same principle can be applied to well-designed storage. A working wall of shelves, for example, can be tailored to store and display all sorts of items, whereas separate storage for different possessions means floor space is crowded with bookcases, magazine racks, cupboards and supports for the stereo units. Well-planned shelving means those items regularly used are within easy reach – and the plan should also include spotlights for highlighting treasured possessions or making it easy to select records or videotapes.

Look for ingenious solutions to make more of the storage space you already have – wire pull-out drawers can dramatically reorganize a wardrobe or pantry; dividing up existing drawers with special inserts or plywood divisions allows small items to be found more easily. The secret of successful storage lies in taking plenty of time both to determine your life-style and to select very carefully the type of furniture that not only suits your personal taste and needs but allows you to make the most of your home and possessions.

When you're looking to buy a house or apartment, one of the most important points to check is a property's storage potential. You really need to carefully assess the space in each room and consider the relationship of one room to another, because storage should relate to how the spaces are used and combined. Top marks go to the architect who designed this split-level home in Germany. Its layout perfectly illustrates the principles of good interior planning. Rooms are divided not by walls but by an open-plan pine wood storage system which echoes the timber construction of the house and blends with the quarry-tiled floors on each level. The kitchen/breakfast room is situated on a level just above this dining room, a family living area is on the floor below and, under that, a children's playroom. All the floors are linked together by short runs of open-plan stairs.

# ONE-ROOM LIVING

First homes, studios or apartments, tend to be small for financial reasons, but provide the challenge of finding the best ways to organize your possessions. Bright and ingenious ideas make all the difference when you are faced with the restraints of living and sleeping in a single room or tiny apartment. Regardless of the total space, a sense of order is achieved if different areas are identified, even if one area has more than one function.

An advantage of living in a restricted space is that it is easier to keep clean, but only if kept reasonably tidy. Lots of clutter in a disorganized room is tiresome to live with, but worse, it makes the room seem smaller than it actually is.

### Serving your needs
Economy is a great asset, in your day-to-day needs and in the number of possessions you acquire when space is limited. Plan storage on the basis of what you really need, not in anticipation of what you might eventually own. The things you do have often provide solutions for the things you don't. If you make pastry only occasionally, a rolling pin is an unnecessary expense and an awkward item to store, but it can be improvised from a strong, straight-sided tumbler. Work out what can serve a dual function and plan your menus around what you have; borrow or hire, if necessary, extra pans and dishes to cater for the occasional large dinner party. Bulk-buying of groceries may make economic sense, but has practical restrictions. Organize a few friends and neighbors to share the bargains, so you benefit from the low cost without being encumbered with enormous quantities.

The kitchen can be confined within a space equivalent to a walk-in cupboard. A single sink covered with a chopping board makes a tiny work surface and very little space is needed alongside for a two-ring electric burner unit. A well-ventilated kitchen alcove obscured by a blind or screen is out of sight and out of mind when not in use.

If the kitchen area is left open, arrange the trestle table so that one end becomes the kitchen worktop, the other extending into the living area and kept clear for dining or working. Tabletop appliances – a mini-oven or microwave –

One-room living often demands ingenious solutions to make the most of a limited space and conventional furniture usually just doesn't give the sort of flexibility that is needed to make a space work for both sleeping and living. Here, a huge wooden platform serves as a casual seating unit, large enough for three or four to sit comfortably with space provided for books and a stereo. At night, a bed base on castors pulls out like a giant drawer from beneath the platform. Another smaller drawer on the left is used for storing duvet and pillows. An old pine wardrobe keeps all clothes sensibly in one place and, as wall space is minimal, mirrors, cut to size, fit in its two center panels. The all-white walls and floor visually enlarge the space and the plants which thrive in this light, sunny room were deliberately chosen because their tall, thin shapes are less space-restricting than those types which tend to grow wide and bushy.

are big enough to cook for a modest dinner party, small enough to put away on a wide shelf or at the back of a cupboard. Fit extra shelves into recesses or at the side of a wall-mounted cupboard. Use every inch of space you have, screw hooks on the back of a door for tea towels and saucepans. When you buy kitchen items, consider how they can be stored. Much modern tableware is designed to be neatly stacked, a space-saving asset. Three high quality kitchen knives are a better investment than a full set of inferior ones, and the same goes for saucepans.

The bathroom may be the only separated space in studio accommodation, and is likely to be minute. Keep storage to a bare minimum; if possible within the bathroom, protected behind tight-fitting waterproof doors. Keep towels, robes and laundry bag on hooks screwed into the door. Wire-grid systems or plastic stacking trays, accessible, durable and clean, provide storage space for essentials such as soap, toothbrush, sponge and razor.

### Between waking and sleeping

The initial outlay on a well-designed bed is a worthwhile investment. It is the most important piece of furniture in one-room living, but it probably has to serve as seating too, converted to a sofa when covered with a bright bedspread and piled with cushions. A good quality sofabed is a wise purchase, and many designs now incorporate drawers in the base. If you dismantle the bedding during the day, you can pack it neatly into the base; otherwise, this provides extra space for clothing or clean sheets and towels.

The bed necessarily occupies a proportion of the floor space, but avoid conventional furniture such as a wardrobe and chest of drawers, which intrude on the room and further restrict your movements. Arrange a wall of adjustable shelving, where you can store clothes folded or hung up. Conceal it with mirrored doors to give a greater feeling of space, or fit it with blinds to match those at the windows.

At ground level, there are ways of visually dividing the room into separate living and sleeping areas, using simple screens or freestanding storage. A tall bookcase can separate

the "bedroom" from the daytime space, with access to its contents from both sides. Sturdy, brightly colored modular units can serve the same function, open on both sides for easy access or backed to seal off the different areas. You can add to these units as your budget permits, to accommodate new possessions or further divide the space.

An extra-high ceiling can provide an opportunity for split-level sleeping or living. A mattress on a raised platform supported by hefty scaffolding opens up what would otherwise have been wasted space. The recess beneath can be adapted to your particular requirements. A wide worktop and bookshelves can be installed here, or you can fit up

*Left: A simple modular shelving system and a bright curtain create varied divisions between areas without permanently enclosing or reducing any of the space in this tiny studio.*

*Below: This ingenious storage system virtually divides a room and provides open shelving, desk space and two wardrobes which are concealed from the living area.*

simple cubbyholes and shelves out of natural or painted timber, to store clothing and shoes or the paraphernalia of practical pastimes, for example, art materials or a sewing machine. You can put clothes on a hanging rail slung beneath the sleeping platform and curtain off the space. This neatly encapsulates an area for sleeping and dressing.

A sturdy platform constructed at table-height across one end of the room marks off a place for work or sleep, with low-level storage underneath. The ingenious futon is eminently suitable for one-room living; whether laid on the floor or on a platform, it is easily rolled up and tucked completely out of sight. It can alternatively be placed on a

movable plain wooden base, fitted with drawers or cupboard doors. Push the base against the wall and roll up a second futon at the back to make a comfortable sofa; a spare futon is also, effectively, a spare bed when rolled out on the floor.

Obtain versatile furniture or simple, inexpensive items that you can rearrange as necessary. A table can be made from a worktop placed across two trestles. This doubles as a practical desk as well as a dining table and can be stacked away when not in use. The worktop can equally well rest on two small cupboards or filing cabinets. A low filing cabinet on wheels makes a useful bedside table with space for storing clothes; it is easily moved to the side of a chair or sofa.

# KITCHENS

The kitchen is usually the greediest area for storage, demanding not only sufficient space for a vast and diverse range of equipment and edibles, but also in specific places if the room is going to have any sense of order about it. It is easier to find room for everything if your kitchen is well designed and thoroughly planned from the outset. Good looks are, of course, an important aspect but efficient function, safety and economy of movement must be worked into the scheme too.

Planning or simply reorganizing a kitchen involves a network of decisions and you need to give a great deal of thought to how and what you like to cook in order to achieve the sort of kitchen in which you'll feel at home. The best way to tackle the situation is to consider the position of the basic elements: sink, stove and refrigerator. The tried and tested formula for an efficient and safe work pattern between major items is: prepare; cook; serve/prepare; clean; prepare. This pattern can take the form of one unbroken line or a closely related "working triangle."

**Planning a kitchen layout**
As a rule of thumb, this work sequence should be confined to a space of between 12 feet and 22 feet, incorporating enough storage space for all the materials and utensils needed there. These are the essentials of a good, safe working kitchen even if the only cooking you do is to make tea. If space is tight you would do better to consider making room elsewhere for laundry and cleaning equipment, deep freeze and occasional or bulk storage.

The following sequences show how the working triangle can be arranged – the one best suited to you is likely to depend on the size and shape of your kitchen.

**In-line layout** The simplest arrangement is a single line with everything set against a suitable wall. This sequence is ideal for long narrow rooms or one wall of a studio apartment where the kitchen could be screened off by sliding or folding doors. The most practical sequence is worktop, sink, worktop, range, worktop, kept within a span of about 20 feet.

## Safety

**DO**
- keep chemicals out of children's reach.
- keep a fire blanket and extinguisher by the stove.
- provide adequate lighting over work areas.
- use steps to reach high shelves or cupboards.

**DON'T**
- interpose a traffic route between oven and sink.
- place burners near curtains and blinds.
- fix cupboards over burners.
- let cupboard doors clash with opening room doors.
- position electrical sockets too near sinks and burners.
- interrupt worktop runs with full-height units.

*Don't be deceived by this romantic, nostalgic kitchen; it has been planned to incorporate all the essential modern conveniences. The rustic beam above the stove conceals lighting and extractor fan, the deep recess provides ample hanging space for utensils. Recessed downlights illuminate the pretty display of china on the dresser.*

**Galley layout** The galley kitchen has two parallel runs with sink and stove on one side, food storage, including refrigerator, and preparation areas on the other. It is an easy layout to work with but the corridor needs to be around 4 feet wide if there's more than one cook; for a single person this gap can be reduced to 2½ feet. This layout is not advisable if the central aisle is a main thoroughfare with doors at both ends.

**U-shaped and L-shaped layouts** In these layouts the "working triangle" falls into its natural sequence between either two or three walls and is compatible for both small and large kitchens. In larger rooms the essential triangle should still be kept within the optimum span.

In a kitchen/dining room, one side of the "U" or "L" can form a peninsula and visually make the dividing line between the two areas. To emphasize this, the dividing worktop can be split into two levels; a lower counter on the kitchen side with a wide shelf above. This usefully doubles as a serving counter and casual snack bar, also helping to conceal the kitchen when dining is more formal.

**Island layout** This is a layout favored by serious cooks and best suited to large rooms. A central work station houses the stove and, if space and finances permit, an extra sink for food preparation. This work station may also become a dining table, or at least a place where family or friends can sit around and watch the cook at work, and it provides an attractive focal point to the room.

### Kitchen storage

Having worked out a suitable layout, plan how materials and utensils can be stored in relation to the work zones where they are first needed, and where they can be logically returned. Putting things back in place is a chore that even modern technology hasn't yet resolved, but with common sense you can make it relatively quick and easy. Sometimes good planning obviates the need to put everything away, and attractive items can be displayed.

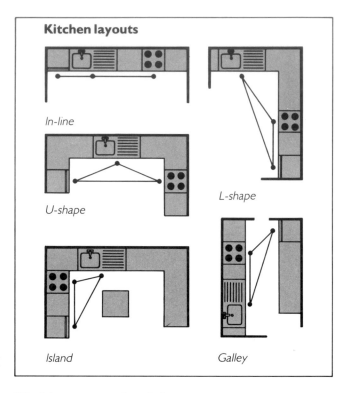

**Kitchen layouts**

*In-line*

*U-shape*

*L-shape*

*Island*

*Galley*

### Washing zone – the sink

If space permits a double sink is best, particularly for the busy cook. One bowl can be covered with a chopping board and when food preparation is finished, the washing up is done in one bowl, rinsed and drained in the other. In a tight space a single sink can be freed to work if the washing up is left to drain on a rack above it. It's not only hygienic and saves drying up, the rack provides practical storage for everyday china, especially if hooks are fitted to hold cups and mugs.

If you prefer to keep everything behind closed doors, china can drain on a rack hidden away inside a bottomless wall cupboard. Ensure that the cupboard is hung in a position that allows the drips to go into the sink, not down the wall or onto the floor.

A rubbish bin of appropriate size needs to be close to the sink; housed in a long, deep drawer beneath the worktop, it leaves both your hands free to scrape plates or scoop vegetable peelings from sink to bin.

Any plumbed-in appliances are economically housed near

*Left: A simple wooden drainer is designed so that dishes can drip dry and be stored in one place, conveniently above the sink. Baking tins used only occasionally are kept higher up on the rack. Glass shelves are held safely in place by special brackets with upturned lips and the mirrored wall visually enlarges this narrow galley kitchen. Cutlery is kept well organized in old ceramic mustard jars.*

*Above: A wooden grid is suspended from the ceiling and makes a practical solution for storing mis-matched utensils, drying herbs and the cook's string of garlic.*

*Far left: An industrial wire grid used for the reinforcement of cement structures has been adapted to make a display of kitchen utensils, simply attached by butchers' hooks.*

*Left: End of unit shelves make china easily accessible.*

*Below: A stove is given a canopied exhaust hood, neatly disguised.*

the sink. You may not consider a dishwasher top priority, but it's a very hygienic method of washing up and saves time on a boring job.

Washing machines were traditionally housed in kitchens before technology developed automatic programming. From the point of view of hygiene, they are really incompatible with the kitchen and are far more logically installed in a utility area. Modern designs have the advantage of space-saving features such as washing machine and tumble-dryer combined.

Detergent and pan scourers should be within easy reach of the sink and these can neatly fit into a rack hung inside a cupboard door. Cleaning items used less frequently need not be stored here. Space beneath the sink, particularly if it's on an outside wall, can easily be ventilated to provide a cool, dark larder for vegetables conveniently close to hand.

Drying cloths on telescopic towel rails fit neatly into a narrow cupboard or gap beneath the worktop, often a space where trays of awkward shape and large chopping boards can also be stacked.

## Cooking zone – oven, stove or combination

In a large family kitchen the "split-level" separate oven and stove is a practical choice. Oven, grill and microwave can be moved out of the "working triangle" and built into a tall housing unit where they're out of reach of children but on eye level for the cook. Heavy pots and casseroles are safely stored beneath the ovens and a heat-resistant glove should be within easy reach. Near the stove you need to store all the items used during cooking – that includes herbs, seasonings and stirring utensils as well as saucepans and frying pans.

In smaller kitchens a combined stove with built-in oven is more space-saving. Remember to allow 1 foot of heat-resistant worktop, preferably on both sides of the stove.

Whatever the size of your kitchen a modern essential is an exhaust hood fitted over the stove. There are two types – one recycles air through a charcoal filter, the other, more efficient type, removes smoke and steam through a vent pipe to the outside, leaving the kitchen free from lingering food smells and damaging condensation.

**Preparation zone – refrigerator**

The size and type of refrigerator you need largely depends on how and what you eat. Fresh foods, other than dairy and meat products, appreciate a less cool temperature and many new designs for fridges now incorporate three zones – larder, refrigerator and deep freeze – to keep the various contents in peak condition. A well-designed refrigerator should use every scrap of space for maximum efficiency and energy-saving, and that includes adjustable shelving both inside the cabinet and on the back of the door. If you are having the refrigerator built in, be sure that it can be adequately ventilated from behind or has a top-mounted venting, and site it well away from other appliances that generate heat.

Food stuffs not kept in the fridge or freezer should be stored in close proximity to the preparation zone for easy access. Pull-out pantry cupboards filled with adjustable shelves make everyday basics clearly visible and easily accessible from both sides. Conventional base units can be fitted with wire baskets on runners to save you from groping in the back of dark cupboards. In a narrow galley kitchen, wide, open shelves and a couple of low, deep drawers make more accessible storage than conventional cabinets.

Different types of surfaces are needed for preparing food – wooden boards for chopping, marble slabs for pastry-making. They can be built into the worktops themselves; if separate, they take up less space standing vertically or slid into a shallow shelf under wall units. Some sophisticated kitchens have pull-out worktops to increase counter space.

Food preparation counters must be kept squeaky clean, and this is made easier if they are kept free of clutter. Use the wall space immediately above worktops for hanging utensils either on fixed rods or on individual hooks. A wire grid system is a versatile method for storing kitchen paper holders, spice racks and other small accessories.

A good set of super-sharp kitchen knives is a basic essential and for easy food preparation they should be kept in peak condition. Mounted on a magnetic rack, or slid into a wooden block or slots cut into the back of a worktop, they are

*Far left: A galley kitchen is an easy layout to work with but safest when access is restricted to one end. A well-lit alcove recess between cupboards is just the right width for storing tabletop appliances and books.*

*Above left: Kitchen units do not have to be of a uniform width. Thin pull-out drawers make contents easily visible and accessible. The lower section keeps oddly shaped bottles safely upright.*

*Below left: A narrow hinged box pulls out and conveniently stores long French loaves and sharp knives. Lined with a plastic sack, this same unit would also make a practical rubbish bin.*

instantly accessible. If you prefer to keep them out of sight, a separate section should be reserved in a drawer, away from other cutlery and utensils but close to the sharpener.

Above the worktop lightweight items can stand on open shelves or in cupboards. Shelving is cheaper and shows off attractive packaging, jars and everyday china but shelves should be limited to about 8 inches deep for easy reach. Cupboards suit the less tidy-minded but still need to be organized with items used regularly at the front and those used less often at the back. The inside face of a wall-cupboard door is often wasted and can be fitted with hooks, racks, narrow shelves, foil and plastic wrap dispensers – but don't overload it.

Small electrical appliances are energy-saving and make the

*Far left: Small kitchens look more spacious if colors and accessories are kept simple.*

*Left: Even a tiny kitchen can house a breakfast bar.*

cook's life easier, but gadgets become gimmicks unless regularly used. An electric coffee-grinder tucked away in a cupboard means you'll soon resort to the instant or ready-ground varieties. Make sure you have enough electrical sockets at worktop height.

## How to plan a kitchen

Draw a diagram of the room on graph paper using a sensible scale – 1:20 is practical – and don't forget to mark positions of doors, windows, electrical sockets, radiators, etc. Make scaled cutouts of the appliances you have and are keeping, and of those you intend to buy.

Many kitchen manufacturers and retailers offer a free planning service, but they too will need all the above information. Their advice may prove invaluable, giving you ideas and suggestions you would never have thought of, but the kitchen must be studied carefully. Remember, too, they are in the business of selling kitchen furniture, so don't be fooled into thinking you need all that they'd like to sell you.

## Vertical layout

Kitchen units and appliances are standardized at a height of 2 feet 11 inches which discriminates unfairly against very tall or short people. Well-designed units have adjustable plinths; those that don't can be removed entirely or raised to a more suitable height. Built-in toe space of at least 3 inches makes it easier to reach the back of worktops and wall cupboards.

Food preparation worktops should have at least a ¾ inch overhang of base units to make it easier to sweep off crumbs, vegetable peelings and so on. The standard depth of worktop, 2 feet, is not really broad enough and a little extra depth provides useful storage in the preparation zone. Worktops do not have to be all on the same level; washing up is easier at a slightly higher level than jobs such as rolling pastry and chopping vegetables. The right height is what feels right for you.

Wall cupboards should be mounted at least 1 foot 4 inches above worktops and 180-degree hinges or up-and-over doors prevent the risk of banging your head.

**Plan for a kitchen**

**Plan view and front elevation**

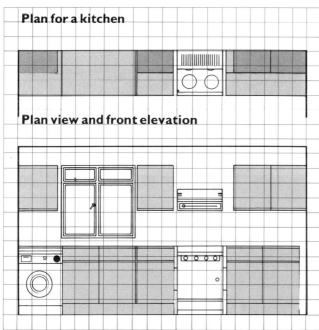

# DINING ROOMS

Delicious food, an imaginatively decorated table, intimate lighting and gentle music are the ingredients for successful entertaining. How and what you eat is much more important than where you eat – a relaxed, comfortable atmosphere puts both you and your guests at ease, whether you dine in the kitchen, living or dining room, or even in the hall.

Preparing food should be a joy not a chore, but the less confident or inhibited chef may feel more relaxed if formal dining is kept apart from the cooking operation. A room reserved solely for dining is an expensive waste of space and in most homes the room in which meals are taken almost certainly has a dual role.

### Living and dining

A combined living and dining room is a very popular option and the dining area can be partitioned off by folding doors, a screen or a room divider mainly consisting of shelving. The room may be too small to take a permanent, full-sized dining table comfortably, but there's a wide choice of designs with extension leaves or flaps that fold out, or you can opt for the simple trestle version that's put up only when you need it and is otherwise stored neatly away. Folding chairs that also store flat will stop the room from looking overcrowded.

### Kitchen/diners

The added bonus of an attractive, well-planned kitchen is that you'll almost certainly want to eat there, too. Even if you have a separate dining room, some meals are just more conveniently eaten in the room where the food is prepared. Gone are the days when the cook was banished to the kitchen to churn out endless meals single-handed, joining the dining table in between tending to the different courses. Meal times are far more relaxed and sociable occasions when the opportunity to meet and talk is as important as the meal itself.

Unless your kitchen is fitted into a cupboard there's always a way to find space for somewhere to sit and eat. Some kitchen designs incorporate retractable dining tables within base units; a cheaper alternative is to mount a large hinged shelf on a wall where it can be folded down when not in use.

Nothing matches exactly but everything blends beautifully in this elegant dining/kitchen room. By stopping the run of the fitted kitchen units, and using a different, freestanding style of furniture to store china and glass, the two areas of the room are emphatically separated. The shelves of an otherwise formal cabinet have been softened by the sensitive addition of fabric.

Left: To appreciate the delicate patterns on china plates, they are best displayed upright. As a safety measure, fix a wood bar along the back edge of shelves to prevent them slipping or toppling over. This display is deliberately arranged so that regularly used china is to the front and on lower, more accessible levels.

Right: The dining table is the center of attention in this French kitchen. An entire wall of units is devoted to serving food and storing china and glass. Plates, too old to eat from, make a pretty display. A row of wall spots, used as uplights, provides good, but diffused, light.

An instant breakfast bar is made by combining a simple worktop with narrow stools or folding chairs.

In busy family kitchens, it's wise to keep young children out of the cooking and preparation zones, but still confined within the room where you can keep an eye on them. A run of low-level units forming a peninsula divides the kitchen practically and safely. The counter provides a serving area and additional tabletop. Sensible designs include cupboards with doors that open on both sides, so items such as china and glass can be taken to the table from one side and returned, via the sink, from the other.

Storage of china, cutlery and glass should be planned according to how and when they are used. Everyday items are most practically kept near the sink, so they can be put away effortlessly; precious glasses, silver and dinner services reserved only for special occasions need not be stored here at all. China and glass that are rarely used make a beautiful and almost permanent decorative display on the open shelves of a dresser or behind the dust-proof protection of glass doors.

Tabletop appliances, such as the toaster and coffee-maker, are appropriately placed near the dining table, to save you getting up to refill cups or hovering around the grill. Jams, sauces, spreads and condiments need to be kept together somewhere near the serving and preparation zones. A narrow cupboard or shelves at the end of a peninsula puts them equidistant between the two.

### Dining rooms

If a separate room is used regularly for dining, make sure it's well heated, close to and on the same level as the kitchen. This room, permanently equipped with a sizeable, sturdy table, is also ideal for homework, hobbies and sewing. The amount of storage you need depends on your interests and equipment, of course, but allow sufficient space to conceal the typewriter, computer or sewing machine as well as the china, cutlery and glass needed for dinner parties. A con-

ventional sideboard takes up a lot of space and offers limited storage. A dresser combining concealing cupboards and display glass cabinets gives good vertical storage; it may come in two parts, one sitting on top of the other. If the glass cabinet at the top can be wall-mounted, the flat-topped cupboard below makes a useful sideboard.

A practical way of combining extra seating with permanent storage is to build in a fitted cupboard the length of the table, the height and depth of a chair seat. Add seat and back cushions and you have a comfortable bench with lots of hidden space to store things below.

If the room is only occasionally used it will probably be cooler than the rest of the house and can provide space at the right temperature for storing your wine. Keep the bottles in simple wood or metal wine racks, sufficiently portable to be moved out if you are heating the room for any length of time.

Preparing food in advance leaves you free to entertain guests and a mobile heated trolley may be worth considera-

tion. You will have to adapt your cooking techniques slightly and choose your menu with care, as most food suffers from being kept hot. Vegetables should be undercooked as they'll continue cooking in a hot cabinet, whereas roast meats appreciate a "set" time of about fifteen minutes before carving.

A wide, fixed shelf at table height with electric sockets above forms a serving counter where you can plug in hot trays, plate warmers or an electric wok for stir-frying on the spot. The shelf doubles as a desk or worktop when needed for other pursuits. A mobile bar with an integrated refrigerator provides a separate place to serve drinks and to keep cold desserts chilled until serving.

If the room overlooks a garden or balcony, more adventurous cooks can make space for a barbecue and enjoy *al fresco* food nearly all year round. Whatever its aspect, put on some relaxing music, light the candles or lower the light above the table, and you're dining in style.

# LIVING ROOMS

A living room should be the easiest room to plan and organize – the only constraints are your budget and the available space. But it is that freedom, in terms of style and type of furnishings, that makes decisions the more perplexing.

A further complication is a certain ambiguity of function. In the past, houses were built with a front parlor reserved for "best" and a back room for everyday living. Now the two have been combined: the living room is the showpiece of a home, the area most frequently seen by outsiders, but also the room that you come home to for total relaxation in privacy and comfort. Other rooms make more stringent demands with regard to function and practicality. Large appliances in the kitchen often dictate how space may be most economically used; so, too, do bathroom fixtures and bedroom furniture. But the living room gives you a free hand to create exactly what you and your family want, according to your life-style. The danger here is that it is tempting to gloss over the importance of planning the layout, and rush straight into color schemes and soft furnishings. Storage is often an afterthought, but together with lighting and heating, it forms an important and integral part of a relaxing, easy and comfortable room. These three basic aspects should be considered together.

Central heating is now a modern essential rather than a luxury; if a system is well planned, with good, flexible controls, it can have more effect than any other home improvement. Standard radiators do have limitations – most are visually unappealing and take up valuable wall space. There are designs which run the length of walls at skirting level, which are less obtrusive and free the walls above for built-in storage or simple shelving. A conventional radiator can be disguised by painting it the same color as the walls. A shelf, the same width and depth as the radiator, fixed about 4 inches above it, can be used to display attractive objects, drawing attention away from the less attractive radiator beneath. If it is close to a window this shelf makes an ideal home for tropical plants, given sufficient humidity. Radiators can be moved or changed for more efficient types or sizes and this is a worthwhile consideration if the installation you

A large living room gives ample proof that combining several functions in one room need not lead to chaos or lack of style. Good natural light has been maximized by using thin, translucent blinds that give privacy without restricting any light. The radiator beneath the window is cunningly concealed by an open-slat wood frame, so it functions efficiently but invisibly. Storage is not confined to the handsome pine cupboard but discreetly added under the built-in seating. Upholstery fabric matches the blinds to minimize distractions of color or the space-reducing effect of patterns. Generous, casual shelves contain the family collection of books. The room can be transformed from daytime playroom to adult living room in minutes.

*Economy is no bar to style: by using one color for all components of this living room, and by reducing decoration to a handful of well-displayed objects, a simple elegance is achieved. An illusion of space is enhanced by inserting the alcove shelves into the wall before finish-plastering, for a cantilevered look, by rejecting a traditional fireplace in favor of a simple recessed type.*

have inhibits a room's heat efficiency or makes a sensible storage layout impossible.

### Using the space

Really spacious living rooms are a joy in summer but can be freezing expanses in winter. Sometimes it is wiser to accommodate these seasonal weather changes rather than fight them. Furniture chosen for flexibility offers the opportunity to move seating further into the room when it is colder so that storage such as bookcases and modular units can be put against outside walls for added insulation. A large room may also be partitioned in winter with freestanding storage. Make use of the window side during the day, when it's warmer, and retreat to the other side of the divider at night, where the space can be heated more easily.

Smaller living rooms are naturally cosy; the problem here is how to, visually at least, gain space. Avoid large pieces of dark heavy furniture that tower overhead. If you install shelving, only fit it to the depth you actually need and if possible restrict storage to one wall or limited area. Shelves always look

better grouped together, giving the impression of being planned rather than merely thrown up at random. Store only what you really need to have easily at hand or want to display, in order to leave more space free for comfortable and generous seating.

Older homes have fireplaces which once made natural focal points to the rooms; and although the fireplace may not house the heat source any more, it is still likely to be an attractive feature. The mantelpiece is tailormade for display. An uplighter concealed in the fireplace itself accentuates a beautiful surround and highlights plants standing in the grate. On either side of the chimney breast, alcoves give scope for considerable storage. Display shelves are easily built within each space and doors fixed to lower shelves combine concealed with open storage. In traditional or period style rooms, visually incompatible equipment such as sound systems, the television and video may look better behind closed doors. Deeply spaced shelves that pull out on runners allow more flexibility in the positioning of the television, with the video recorder above or below it.

*Without visible means of support, these glass shelves seem to float against the walls of the alcoves. Careful choice of the material for the shelf itself enhances a display.*

## Permanent storage

When building shelves or units to house electrical equipment, remember to consider the positions and capacity of electrical outlets. Overloaded adaptors are dangerous and, if sockets are at base board height and the stereo at waist-level, there will be trailing wires that must be kept unentangled and concealed.

Good modern storage for home entertainment is gradually emerging but many designs have severe limitations. Units built to house a television and video have little, or unsuitable, space for tapes; audio storage often allows room for thirty albums and no more, completely ignoring a section for cassettes. Collections always expand and many expensive units have almost built-in redundancy.

Speakers, a vital part of any sound system, need careful positioning if they're to be effective; one day, perhaps, architects will start planning homes with built-in facilities for concealing them. Until then, we have to improvise and find places at the right height with sufficient space between for reasonable sound balance. Speakers should never be placed directly on the floor where part of the sound is absorbed and can annoy neighbors beneath.

Living-room storage can contribute to making space for casual meals. The ubiquitous coffee table, though handy, is much more useful when it features low-level shelves or compartments. Magazines and books are quickly stored below, clearing the top for plates and cups. Cube storage is ideal for this purpose and can be moved easily; combine several cubes to make one large, low table or use single or paired units as perfect one-place settings.

Whatever you are storing or displaying needs careful positioning in the room. Central heating can be damaging; protection can be provided by a correct-output humidifier, which puts sufficient moisture back into the air to counter the heating's drying effect. Avoid putting anything made of wood too close to a radiator or in strong, direct sunlight; audio and video cassettes can also be badly affected by excess heat or light. Ornaments on display near a window should be regularly moved or they will leave marks on the surface.

# BEDROOMS

In the bedroom comfort is top priority, and the atmosphere should be relaxing and secure. Your bed is the only essential piece of furniture here and many people would find their sleep, and perhaps the quality of their lives, dramatically improved by investment in a new bed.

Apart from improving your state of health, a new bed can also provide useful storage. Many designs have drawers built into the bed base, or cupboards and shelving integrated with the headboard. Some modern mattresses offer enough support to be used without a bed base, either placed directly on the floor or on a platform or solid base which could be designed to incorporate a series of drawers. A bed raised high off the floor can be fitted with cupboards acting as low-height wardrobes. These options are well worth considering when you are planning to furnish or reorganize a bedroom; tailormade furniture like this, combining both sleeping platform and storage, may be less expensive than the cost of a conventional bed and individual pieces of storage furniture.

Another good idea is the futon, the Japanese sleeping mat, a firm, thin mattress which is rolled up during the day and spread out only at night. Ideal for back sufferers, this solid mattress made from layers of plump cotton can be left permanently flat, but must rest on a base which allows air to circulate around it. This base could still be used to incorporate neat, concealed storage.

We spend an incredible third of our lives in bed. This includes time spent not actually sleeping but reading, eating or merely relaxing. Space is needed to cater to these additional comforts. Bedside tables are usually ridiculously small and totally inadequate for books, magazines, radio and breakfast tray, and too low for convenient placing of a reading lamp. Shelves above the bed, positioned so you don't bang your head when sitting up, make an ideal support for a swivel reading light. They can also house speakers, if you like bedtime music, and you can easily reach for books and magazines without getting out of bed. A mobile storage unit at the end of the bed makes a convenient space for television and video; wheel it round the bed to make a table.

Hanging space is not the only requirement for bedroom storage. Many people use the room for relaxing, reading, watching television, besides the more expected activities of sleeping and dressing. These alcoves have been well planned to cope with a multitude of requirements: drawers below hold small items of clothing (wardrobes often lack this), wider shelves hold ornaments and adjustable reading lights, while higher shelves of usefully varied sizes hold books. Both cupboards can be screened by pulling down blinds that match those at the window and the color of the bedcover.

## Organizing the space

If floor space is tight, don't be tempted to skimp and make do with a smaller bed in order to make room for other items; too much furniture in a small room will make it appear claustrophobic and cluttered. A bedroom is experienced in both darkness and light; masses of furniture towering around the bed can form an uncomfortable presence not conducive to easy, restful sleep. Before choosing other furniture, consider the outlook from the bed position and make sure there will be enough space to get in and out with ease. If the room is really tiny, rather than filling it up so it looks smaller still, consider installing cupboards outside or turning another room close by into a dressing room.

Freestanding furniture does provide flexibility in a bed-room, which can be advantageous if you like reorganizing the room to suit the time of year. A bed positioned beneath an open window may be delightful in summer, but in winter it will be cosier pushed up against an internal wall. Many ranges of freestanding bedroom furniture are designed to seem built-in and storage intended for other parts of the house often looks equally at home in the bedroom.

If you have certain pieces of furniture – antiques or senti-mental heirlooms perhaps – that feel right in the bedroom but cannot be matched with a wardrobe of suitable size, improvise with a simple screen around a dress-shop clothes rail. This offers a temporary and sympathetic stop-gap while you continue the search for just the right item.

Neat built-in storage takes up less floor space than free-

shelves or retained within small sections. If you have a huge collection they may be better off in a blanket box. If it has an upholstered top or is covered by a cushion, it doubles up as simple bedroom seating.

Restricted space for clothes can be utilized efficiently by dividing clothes into winter and summer wardrobes. Out-of-season clothes are packed away in suitcases or zipped bags made of tough plastic, kept on the highest wardrobe shelves, under the bed or in a different room altogether.

When clothes are stored in cupboards of any kind, don't overlook the potential of fitting inside surfaces with hooks where you can hang belts and jewelery. Two screw eyes or hooks linked together with a fine rod or thin elastic make a simple tie or scarf rack.

Silver belts and necklaces do not appreciate exposure to the air and will quickly tarnish, so are better kept in boxes with tightly fitting lids. Tiny and precious jewels are safer in boxes, too. Office stationers have all sorts of containers constructed of swivel trays, pots and boxes of various types and in various combinations. Suitable sizes make storage for jewelery and cosmetics.

The dressing table is the traditional home for smaller and more personal things, but a similar arrangement may be easily improvised. A wide shelf fixed at table height with narrower shelves above and on either side of a suitable mirror also forms a neat study area or writing desk. The small shelves can be painted or covered with fabric to match the color scheme, the large shelf acting as the tabletop protected by a piece of finished glass made secure with clips at the edges. The shelves show off pretty bottles and jars and provide the location for a light angled to illuminate the mirror.

Another inexpensive idea is a wooden or veneered counter placed between two unfinished pine chests of drawers, leaving enough space for a chair or stool so you can sit in front of the mirror. Surfaces can be stained or painted, and finishing details such as knobs and handles, chosen to complement other features in the room, can transform such an arrangement into effective storage that looks just as attractive as a ready-made item.

# BATHROOMS

Fitted kitchens are a standard feature in many new homes, yet bathrooms are for the most part minimal; a bath, washbasin and toilet. And when you think about it, even these few items are not a very happy combination. A separate toilet is more hygienic and especially practical if two or more people share the home.

If a bathroom is small, its function is easier to define. A large room logically makes a laundry, too, and since a basic essential of a bathroom is heat, a washing machine can only contribute to keeping the room warm – but check that installation complies with safety regulations.

Depending on space and the location of the water tank, an airing cupboard is often featured in the bathroom. If possible, it is more practical to have this cupboard opening into the room from outside, as the only regularly used items are towels. An electric rail dries towels and keeps them comfortably warm; this is better than draping them over a radiator, which inhibits it from heating the room efficiently. More economical is a rack which hangs above the radiator, so the towels do not monopolize all the heat. Two curtain-pole brackets and a short length of doweling make a simple, inexpensive rail that can be designed to the length of the radiator or number of towels.

Hand towels should be within easy reach of the basin. Borrow an idea from the kitchen and fit a paper towel holder to the wall or inside the door of a cupboard, or make your own roller towel.

## Concealed storage

Unless you are totally reorganizing a bathroom, storage has to be fitted on either side of and above the bath, basin and toilet. If it is planned well, it also conceals the plumbing. Space is usually wasted around pedestal basins, and in any major improvement you should consider a countertop bowl, which allows you to decide the most convenient height, rather than being dictated to by manufacturers. If you have small children they will need a solid block or box to use as a step up to the toilet or the basin. A countertop basin offers more flexibility in the choice of position, as it is supported by the counter

**Safety**

**DO**

● check that all light fittings conform to safety regulations – if in any doubt check with a qualified electrician.

● keep medicines safely locked away in a purpose-built medicine cabinet.

**DON'T**

● position lights where they can be reached by someone touching a bath, sink or shower tap.

● keep razors, etc. where they can be reached by children.

*A perfect balance between style and function has been achieved in this understated bathroom. The top of the basin unit, incorporating a large drawer for cosmetics, extends out further than the cupboards below so you can sit to remove or apply make-up. A narrow slab of marble runs the length of the mirror and displays glass storage and tooth mugs. Beside the bath, a cupboard the size of a small wardrobe is lined with shelves to keep the surfaces uncluttered and easier to clean, while clean towels are stored in two open shelves at the top.*

it f and not by the wall, and it can be fitted into a corner with s ce beneath for a large, wide, L-shaped cupboard. If space a und is tight, bi-fold doors overcome the problem.

A mirror for shaving and applying make-up takes up siderable wall space if it is of a size that is easy to use; those mbined with cupboards tend to be small and the storage ace is insufficient for the cosmetics, perfumes, after-shave d so on that you may want to keep there. A mirror over e basin and one elsewhere for shaving or make-up leaves om for two people to cope with the early morning rush ore amicably.

Good lighting is essential here – light should shine directly nto the face to avoid unflattering shadows. Rows of bare ulbs have traditionally framed stage dressing-room mirrors and for very good reasons. These naked bulbs give the best

illumination for applying make-up and shaving. If your bathroom is small, extra mirrors or mirror tiles help create the illusion of space, but ensure that the virtually constant view of yourself is seen in the best light, a warm glow from incandescent bulbs rather than the fluorescent type.

Safety is another important consideration. Since the medicine cabinet is conventionally installed here, it should for obvious safety reasons be placed well out of children's reach. Even if you don't have a young family you cannot rule out the possibility of a child using your bathroom; if you do have small children the bathroom can often resemble a field dressing station! Standard medicine cupboards tend to be too small and there is danger if the overspill is stored where small hands can find it or if, when an emergency does occur, the remedy might be found in any number of places.

*Left: These unusual triangular shelves combine convenient storage space with accessibility. A mirrored wall not only adds to the dimensions of the room, but emphasizes the shelf shapes.*

*Below: Double hand basins save frayed tempers in the early morning. The towel rails, well positioned beneath each one, are also the handles of giant drawers for the laundry.*

Though essential, the majority of medicines and first-aid basics are used infrequently and can therefore be considered long-term storage, along with other occasional items such as suntan lotions. Several boxes, with their contents clearly marked, can be stored on the top shelf of a linen cupboard. Items used more frequently such as aspirin, plasters and antiseptic are better kept close to hand. A locking petty-cash box, available at stationers, is a safe and child-proof container.

The gap between door frame and ceiling can provide extra cupboard space for both infrequent essentials and regular supplies of soap, shampoo and toilet paper. Build one yourself or look out for a wall-hung kitchen cabinet. These odd items can be picked up very cheaply in sales. Similarly, a couple of kitchen base units can house a basin sunk into a water-resistant surface, providing space for cosmetics and toiletries on top with generous storage beneath. Again, if there are children in the home, fit safety catches on lower doors if the cupboards are used to store cleaning materials, bleach and disinfectant. Other storage accessories designed for the kitchen work just as well in bathrooms. More efficient use can be made of internal cupboard space with wire drawers fitted on runners under shelves, waste bins and hooks attached to the backs of cupboard doors.

**Display storage**

A tiered vegetable trolley on castors provides mobile storage for bath oils and salts, soaps, shampoos and bathtime toys. One of the versatile wire-grid systems, hung within easy reach of the bath or shower, can be fitted with hooks for flannels and loofahs, wire baskets for soaps and sponges. Glass shelving makes practical and attractive storage; the shelves are easy to clean and visually do not monopolize space. The transparency makes them suitable carriers for pretty bottles and jars or collections of seashells and plants. Many track shelving systems offer special brackets with upturned lips to hold a sheet of glass securely. Upright supports fixed to either side of a window, spanned with several glass shelves, form an ideal showcase for plants.

Most tropical houseplants thrive in the bathroom where the warmth and humid atmosphere comes closest to their natural habitat. In modern bathrooms, waste bins in primary colors make effective containers for large plants. Traditional and period rooms need planters that coordinate with the bathroom's style. Junk china, too unhygienic to use as table-ware, can be turned into elegant cachepots. Small flowering plants look attractive in large cups and saucers. Old-fashioned chamber pots are big enough to hold and conceal several small plastic pots, filled with a variety of patterned and textured foliage, typical of the Victorian preference for deliberate clutter. If the plants are standing near the bath or basin, you can use similar containers, plastic or ceramic, to hold sponges, brushes, bath crystals and so on, and stand these among the plants. Be careful not to place breakable containers where they could be knocked into the bath.

# CHILDREN'S ROOMS

Though child experts often argue the finer points of bringing up children, the majority would agree that children react most happily to attractive and stimulating surroundings. A child's room needs to be a very special place, a personal retreat where he or she can really feel at home. Planned with care, this room can be periodically adapted to suit the growing child, with only minor and inexpensive changes. Wise parents give their children the freedom to dictate their own surroundings, rather than imposing a decorative scheme which will be quickly outgrown. Practical and simple furnishings can also offer fun and fantasy, providing the basics are planned with a good degree of flexibility.

### Early stages

Before you start to design a child's room, consider first its size and location. Children are often allocated the smallest bedrooms or expected to share an average-sized room. With too little space to play in, they will quickly and understandably spread themselves all over the house. Far better to provide a larger room from the start where they can play, entertain friends and later study, do homework and still have space for hobbies. Wherever the room is situated, you can preserve peace of mind in the early years by installing a baby alarm to link it with the rest of the house.

The basic elements of a child's room should be kept simple. Young children need to be warmer than most adults, but don't put in heating appliances that can be knocked over. Space heaters should be guarded, or mounted high on the wall out of reach; thick curtains will help to keep the room cozy. Floorcoverings need to be tough and easily cleaned.

Gloss or vinyl emulsion walls are hardwearing and can be decorated with an ever-changing parade of pictures, drawings, murals and posters. Lighting, too, needs sensitive planning; an overall light fitted with a dimmer switch gives a soft glow for feeding the baby and to reassure young children afraid of the dark. A good work lamp makes a reading and study light, doubling as a bedside lamp.

This practical environment can then be fitted out with good, solid furniture – with resistant surfaces and no nasty

Far left: An ingenious solution for a small children's room: giant shelves give low-level seating and sleeping platforms as well as providing an exciting play area. Thoughtful provision of narrow shelves, making good use of every available space, creates a lively display area for precious objects.

Left: Adjustable shelving is a wise choice for children's rooms, taking games and toys in early years and books later. Those items that need adult supervision are confined to higher shelves. Stacking plastic boxes make the chore of tidying up less time-consuming. All surfaces are wipeable – an important consideration for small children's rooms.

sharp edges – that can be adapted as the room changes from nursery to teenage bedroom. Though a baby may not spend a great deal of time in the nursery room for the first few months, it makes good sense to keep all the things needed for daily care in one place. A full-sized wardrobe with lots of adjustable shelves stores all the supplies of diapers and numerous changes of clothes. Hanging space can be divided into three levels, later into two. A low cupboard makes a practical, safe support for changing a baby. Two bedside chests spanned by a washable worktop are an inexpensive improvisation. All these items will retain their usefulness, whatever the age of the child.

Babies and young children need a great deal of cleaning and having a washbasin in the child's room eases possible congestion in the bathroom. It is convenient for parents while the baby is small and helpful for a rapidly growing toddler. Cleaning teeth can be a long, slow process for beginners and being rushed by older experts is not the best sort of encouragement. A good investment is a mobile unit with swing-out trays and lots of drawers, from office equipment ranges. Standing near the basin, it is practical storage for all the baby's smaller necessities, such as diaper pins, tissues, rinse water, shampoo and talcum powder; later it's useful for games, brushes and paints, and smaller toys.

**Growing needs**
The bed is a priority; a child should not be given a secondhand bed which may be too worn out to give the vital support needed for a young and developing spine. Better than a bad bed is a good quality new mattress which can be put down on the floor or on a solidly built sleeping platform, raised to provide useful storage space underneath. Modern designs of "tower" structures combine a high-level sleeping area with a lower platform making space for a train set or study area, also used as an additional bed when a friend comes to stay. Raised structures are great fun – their versatility extends to providing a theater for puppet shows and plays, with a spotlight clamped to the frame and a blind hung from the upper level. Blinds can also conceal a storage area underneath a platform.

Children are naturally messy and untidy and won't feel happy until they have pulled out every toy and game before starting to play. The speed and ease with which the room can be cleared up depends upon how well you have organized the storage. If you want your children to develop a sense of order, you must first instigate simple methods for them to learn by. Building bricks which only fit their box if arranged with jigsaw precision will become as much an irritation for you as they are for a child, so make things easy for both of you. Giant stacking boxes or plastic crates take mountains of construction sets, dolls and models, with all their accessories. Empty, they too become games in themselves, building into a space station or make-believe castle.

Rows of adjustable shelving provide homes for cuddly toys and favorite dolls, easily adapted to accommodate books and a stereo later. Many children are avid collectors and a wall of shelves displays precious objects such as old bottles, tins or model aeroplanes.

Scaled-down nursery furniture is quickly outgrown, expensive and short-lived unless you are planning lots of children or can pass things on to someone else. Children will happily make do with old or revamped furniture, but don't let the room become a dumping ground littered with cast-offs from the rest of the house. One wise investment is a desk – an old-fashioned school desk can be bought cheaply at an auction or junk shop, and such designs were built to last. Cleaned up and given a fresh coat of varnish, it takes on a new lease of life. There are also a number of modern designs that are compact, well built and practical for all kinds of study. Covered with a blanket, a desk makes a private play space for a toddler; later it comes into its own as a place for painting or quiet reading in which books and materials can be kept tidy.

Children will be encouraged to dress themselves from an early age if clothes are kept within their reach. A large canvas wallhanging with bright fabric patch pockets keeps shoes, socks, tights and underwear neatly and individually stored. Old school or gym lockers given a fresh lick of paint and fitted with shelves can be allocated to each child if the room is shared.

*Left: Small children need more drawer than hanging space: a neat design incorporates both with a sturdy bunk bed. A simple blind covers all clutter when required.*

*Above: Storage systems that a child can manage foster the habits of tidiness. These boxes have strong, easily gripped handles, and help to avoid the irritations of clearing out the area under a bed.*

# WORKROOMS

Working away from work is becoming a way of life for more and more people every year. Some work at home from choice, whether on behalf of an employer or running a small business that doesn't justify the expense of an office. Others have no choice, such as parents with small children who want to continue a career and must divide their time between working and raising a family. For many others, space is needed not for business but for studying to further their education or pursuing a serious hobby.

Whatever the activity, basic requirements include a practical surface, of a size and at a height to suit both the work and worker, a comfortable chair, suitable lighting and, importantly, storage tailored to meet the demands of the job. Peace and quiet are another essential, particularly if the work requires long periods of static concentration. Working from home should be made pleasurable and a bright, attractive environment that's warm and well ventilated is just as important as an efficient and organized space.

Finding a suitable area to fulfill these needs presents a problem in most modern homes where space is usually at a premium. It is important, though, to allocate a specific space or room. A dining room may double up as a sewing room when making clothes is an occasional interest – as a full-time profession it's unworkable in a room that has to be cleared away for dinner every evening. It also helps to decorate and furnish a permanent workroom in a different style to the rest of your home. That way you can "go to work" and close the door on your domestic surroundings.

One solution is to make more of existing space, dividing corners or alcoves in the living room and bedrooms. Another is to double-use space, furnishing a spare bedroom with a sofa bed and making room for an office as well as overnight guests. Sometimes extra space is less obviously available – you must use lateral thinking and perhaps consider making structural alterations. However, by juggling a little with existing rooms, a work area may be found without causing a major disruption or making a large financial commitment. The size and type of space you need is largely dictated by the kind of job you intend to do.

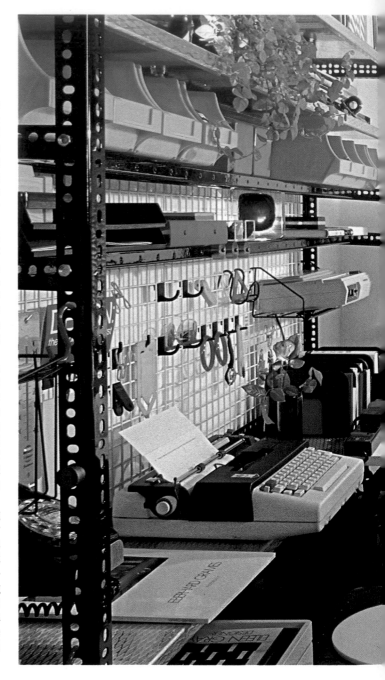

*Left: A well-designed workroom organizes a confined space: the CRT screen is mounted on a pivot at eye level.*

*Below: A home office, designed to work as a dining room too.*

## Home offices and utility rooms

A practical home office can be fitted into the corner of a room, permitting two heights of worktop, one for reading and writing, the other for a typewriter, word processor or computer. Low filing cabinets fit neatly underneath and above the desks, adjustable shelving keeps reference books and files neatly stacked. Filing is a chore in any office, and if it has to be done manually, construct a logical system.

Aim to keep your working area compact but allow enough permanent space and sockets for heavier electrical equipment, which needs to be kept perfectly still and level. Many semi-portable personal computers have built-in disc drives and foldaway keyboards, but even with these space-saving details, you may need to expand your system to include a word processor and printer. The CRT (Computer Display Monitor) could be fixed on a special pivoting arm attached to the wall at a convenient height and position that can be viewed from several directions. Added to all the hardware is the software – cassettes, discs, special paper and manuals. Design the width of your shelving to fit the items being stored, with those regularly used stacked within easy reach from a sitting position. Furniture manufacturers have been slow to respond to the need for media storage, and what there is tends to be overpriced or ill-conceived. It's often a more viable solution to customize conventional furniture or have special units built to your own specifications.

If you're working full time from home it makes sense to create a work space completely different and apart from other rooms. That way you keep your working and leisure hours separate. Sometimes, however, there is an obvious way to dovetail two different functions in one room. Sewing, such as embroidery or tapestry, is a relatively mobile activity needing only a work basket, but if a sewing or knitting machine is to be used frequently, it needs a permanent position with lots of space around for storing materials, cutting out, fitting and pressing. An old pantry or part of a large kitchen can easily be made into a separate laundry incorporating a sewing area. These jobs sit more happily side by side than do preparing food and washing clothes.

*This inspiring room has made use of all the space under the eaves (the units pull out on casters), and by making the most of the windows, avoided a claustrophobic feel.*

A utility room planned in this way needs as much organized storage as a well-run home office and may be furnished in a very similar style. Provide lots of shelving for books, patterns, cleaning materials and small equipment; deep drawer filing cabinets for fabrics and wools; bulletin boards on which to hang notes of measurements and fabric samples. An assortment of different-sized jars or plastic holders hooked to a pegboard makes threads, buttons and zips clearly visible and should be within easy reach from worktops. A long hanging rail or series of wall hooks can be used to air freshly pressed or tumble-dried clothes, and is a convenient place to hang partly made garments. If space is short, an old-fashioned drying rack fixed to the ceiling can be quickly lowered and raised by a simple pulley. More space is saved by an ironing board that retracts into a drawer space, rather than one which is freestanding and needs separate storage when not in use.

## Attics and basements

When assessing the potential of either an attic or basement as a separate workroom, there are three important criteria – access, structure and headroom. An attic with only a hatch opening will need a staircase, and that possibility depends on how much space there is for one on the floor below. As a guide, standard staircases take up a rectangular space of 10 feet by 3 feet, spiral stairs can fit into a space 5½ feet square. Floor joists will probably need strengthening so they can bear the weight of a new room as existing ones would only be adequate for supporting the ceiling below.

To constitute a "habitable" room, headroom of 7½ feet must exist over at least half the floor space. More height can be gained by adding dormer windows instead of roof lights but the cost of this should be weighed up against the potential of the attic as a "non-habitable" room – a store cupboard or extra bathroom.

An area of low loft space can make a delightful play area for children who could then make do with a smaller bedroom, but with sufficient headroom and light a loft makes the ideal painting studio, sewing room or home office. Storage will almost certainly have to be tailormade to make best use of the space under the eaves; pull-out fitted cupboards make that space accessible and at the same time give additional insulation.

At the bottom of a house, access doesn't usually present a problem – gaining sufficient light and ventilation does. A "habitable" room needs a window area at least one-tenth of the floor space. Providing the cellar is free from damp, it may be most practically used as a warehouse for bulk storage. Industrial shelving is easily transported in sections and assembled on site, where it can be used to store anything from wine, bottled preserves and canned food to outgrown toys, decorating equipment and suitcases.

### Workshops

Serious hobbies, such as model-making and furniture design, photography and pottery, demand a whole room if they're to be pursued successfully. The obvious place is a garage or basement where noisy and messy activities are less likely to disrupt the rest of the home. Planning and designing your own workshop needn't be expensive; you can furnish it function-ally, reserving most of your budget for the right tools and equipment. Secondhand kitchen units and tough industrial storage can be customized to suit most needs. Ensure the location has enough electrical outlets for power tools and includes, for added convenience, a water supply.

Good, disciplined storage will help reduce the risk of fire or accidents and keep costly equipment in its best condition. Sturdy adjustable brackets fitted to metal uprights store lengths of timber; single planks make inexpensive shelves where you can keep heavy bottles and tins. The lids of screw-top glass jars can be fitted to the underside of lower planks; the jars, filled with smaller items such as screws and nails, are easily visible and accessible when suspended from a shelf in this way. Odd-shaped tools are less space-consuming if clipped or hooked onto wall-mounted pegboards. A knife rack construction mounted on the back of the work bench safely houses sharp-edged instruments, protecting both their blades and your hands.

As in the kitchen, aim to keep work surfaces clear and uncluttered; but unlike a kitchen, where good looks are a major concern, a workshop is not required to be elegant and the ceiling can be used to provide additional storage space. Pulley systems provide a means of suspending long light-weight ladders, or models which need extensive drying time. A ceiling-mounted track is a flexible system for both light and power, avoiding the danger of trailing wires. Any workshop that stores potentially dangerous chemicals or machinery should be kept locked when not in use.

Where workshops double as garden sheds, special storage needs apply. Seedlings or potted cuttings need slatted shelves for air circulation and water drainage. A concealed spot, a lower shelf, is handy for germinating seeds. Heavy sacks of peat or compost can stand on the floor, but store weed killers or chemicals well out of children's reach. Tools can be hung on the wall to keep them dry and rust-free.

Left: Cleaning equipment, step ladders and hockey sticks often need to be found in a rush and are simply hooked up on the wall of this multi-purpose room.

Right: A home workshop makes simple do-it-yourself jobs much easier because, with a professional start to the task, you're more likely to get a professional finish. And a workshop doesn't have to take up an entire room; if it's well organized, it can easily be confined to a corner of the garage or utility room. Tools need to be accessible and ordered. A pegboard is a cheap solution for this task and keeps things off the floor instead of crammed together in boxes where delicate precision tools are readily damaged. A "work-mate" bench is an essential item but when not in use can be stored high up on the wall, out of the way. Note the jam jars, their lids screwed to the underside of a shelf. Their contents are clearly visible so it's easy to see when you're running short of supplies.

# HALLS

Entrance halls, landings and corridors are often treated as afterthoughts. They are usually the last to be decorated and their potential for useful extra storage or as display areas is often overlooked.

The entrance is where first impressions are made; the welcome it gives reflects on the rest of the house. From a practical point of view, the shape and size of your hall will determine how much space you can steal without interfering with the easy flow of domestic traffic. If both hall and connecting corridor are restricted don't try to take up any of the vital floor space – concentrate on the walls on either side.

In older houses, ugly gas and electricity meters often flaw otherwise attractive areas: if possible make the cupboard run from floor to ceiling when boxing them in. Painted or papered the same as the walls and given a door with a magnetic catch, it can be made to look like a slender column while concealing a long narrow space useful for storing brooms or collapsible chairs.

In narrow hallways, put up rows of coat and hat hooks so you don't get space-consuming and unsightly bulges of clothes piled on top of one another. A bulletin board for messages, cleaning tickets and car keys will be usefully on view as people come in or pass on their way out. If you fix a narrow shelf above a slim radiator it makes a "hall table" as well as preventing warm air from disappearing up the wall.

Long hallways become more interesting if you use them as a picture gallery. Choose your subjects with care, selecting those which don't need to be viewed at a distance, and illuminate them with individual wall lights, a row of adjustable spotlights or downlights recessed in the ceiling. A mirrored panel on one wall creates an illusion of space and reflects the pictures on the opposite wall.

A dead-end corridor can be turned into an efficient storage area, either with floor-to-ceiling display shelves or with the extra space converted to provide a wardrobe and covered by a blind. Mirrored doors will conceal contents and keep them dust-free; they will also visually shorten a long, narrow space, making it more attractive.

High-ceilinged corridors can be improved with the addition of a series of wall-to-wall platforms, leaving sufficient gaps in between to give easy access. Fill these broad shelves with occasionally used, bulky items like the picnic hamper.

Opening up the space understairs can make space for a small dining area and, with intimate lighting focused only above and around the table, you'll disguise the reality of dining in a corridor.

Cupboards fitted below stairs need careful organization or they just become jumbled dumping grounds. The awkward sloping shape makes it difficult to reach the far corners and,

instead of having one large, unmanageable space, it's easier to divide the whole thing into sections. Put each compartment on casters so it can be pulled out independently. Alternatively, open the space at the top; build storage to a comfortable height for seating, leaving space above for a cosy study or telephone snug.

A landing halfway up the staircase can give enough space for low storage and, if it benefits from a sunny outlook, add a window seat for plants or people. Glass shelves across a south-facing window display plants or pretty china.

*Left: This space under the stairs has been divided up exactly to meet the needs of the objects kept there. China and glass are impeccably displayed above a generous sideboard beneath which space is provided for an expanding wine collection, correctly stored horizontally.*

*Above: A broad staircase has been designed to incorporate a library storage system with adjustable shelves to accommodate every size of book. Making a space-divider in this open-plan house, the tiered design doesn't inhibit natural light from reaching all the stairs.*

# ATTENTION TO DETAIL

It's often the tiny details or the simplest of ideas that make an otherwise ordinary storage solution into something rather special. Sometimes it's the finishing touch that makes all the difference. A set of new handles can dramatically change a cheap chest of drawers. Shelves covered with a fabric which coordinates with other soft furnishings mellows the hard edges in a pretty bedroom. Not all fine detailing is merely decorative. A fish bowl filled with multi-colored guest soaps is both attractive and functional; so, too, is a row of aromatic potted herbs along the sill of a kitchen window. The best solutions are frequently the cheapest. Fix light wooden beading on the edges of plankwood shelves or make a simple felt-covered bulletin board to hang small items that would be lost in a capacious cupboard or chest of drawers. Choose and arrange with care and you can make a display of almost anything – colorful beans and seeds in rows of glass jars; dried flowers tied in bunches and suspended from ceilings. And if the objects themselves don't warrant display, then more can sometimes be made of the storage which conceals them. Sturdy cardboard boxes painted or papered merge into the walls on the top of a wardrobe and an old trunk used for storing things used only occasionally makes an additional side-table or extra seating if covered with plump, comfortable cushions.

*Left: A redundant fireplace makes a naturally cool alcove for wine. Brass rods, cut to size, make very elegant supports for deep glass shelves.*

*Below: Thoughtfully framed with deep cubby holes, a window area forms a perfect home office.*

*Bottom left: This rough plank chest was relegated to the garden shed but, sanded and painted, it makes a fine blanket box.*

*Above: Open shelving should be gutsy and deliberate if it's to support beautiful collections with style. The rounded edges of the higher levels are echoed by a deep, solid shelf which is used as a sideboard and conceals drawers.*

*Far left: Saucepans are greedy with space but this tailormade rack stores pans and lids together and spikey wooden arms for hanging mugs and gadgets stick out from both sides.*

*Left: Anyone could make this wooden wall grid, which is more fitting in an old-style kitchen than the metal wire types but no less useful for hanging all manner of small things.*

# PRACTICALITIES

With the variety of convenient materials, easy fixings and lively accessories available these days, it isn't difficult to design some simple additions that make all the difference to your storage facilities. Shelving is versatile, making use of redundant space in a large cupboard or awkward alcove. A recess filled with clutter can be concealed by cupboard doors fitted to a basic wood frame. A facelift for old furniture – new doors on a cupboard or wood stripped down and varnished or painted – brings it back to more years of good life. Small details can be added or exchanged in existing items – knobs, catches, decorative moldings – to give you more enjoyment of storage furniture that looks out of place in new decor or has lost its original appeal.

## Planning the job

If you are putting in new storage of any kind, rather than refurbishing existing furniture, the planning and design of the installation is as important as sound construction methods. Simple shelving is a job that can be tackled without previous experience of doing-it-yourself, but shelves thrown up at random are not much of a home improvement. Even if you have an alcove that seems tailormade for shelving, you are likely to find that the walls are not straight and the corners are not square. You need to place the shelves carefully so they are level and evenly spaced, aligned logically with each other and recessed from the main walls to avoid emphasizing curious angles. Measure the depth and width of the alcove at the shelf heights, as these measurements can vary considerably: if you cut the shelves uniformly, slanting walls can create awkward gaps at either end.

Space the shelves conveniently, so you have easy access to the contents. It is best to put broad, heavy loads at the lower levels with narrow, lightweight display shelving above. When you assemble shelving for books, remember to leave extra space above the height of the books themselves, otherwise they are not easily taken out and replaced.

Whether you are building simple shelves or have ambitions to construct a wall-to-wall cupboard, assemble all the necessary tools and accessories beforehand. For joining

## A basic tool kit

*For most jobs, only very few basic tools are required.*
*Saws – a tenon saw for fine work; a panel saw for the larger scale cuts.*
*Craft knife – better than pencil for cut guidelines.*
*Screwdrivers – a large, medium, and chubby ordinary screwdriver, and one for phillips-head screws.*
*Hammer – a "Warrington". The cross-peen is for driving pins and small nails.*
*Electric drill – a 2-speed*

*model with a set of twist drills, plus a masonry bit.*
*Flexible steel tape – for measuring up.*
*Combination square – more versatile than a try-square, this gives right angles, and doubles as a miniature builder's spirit level.*
*Spirit level – a butcher's level will test verticals and horizontals, and doubles as a straightedge. Alternatively, get a small ordinary level, plus plumb-line and bob.*

sections of wood together, you need joint blocks or corner brackets, screws of the right gauge and length to fit them, and a screwdriver that in turn fits the recess in the screw head. If you are sawing planks and boards to length, a sharp, sturdy saw is the obvious necessity, but you will also need a rigid steel rule or measure so you can repeat measurements accurately – fabric and plastic tape measures are liable to stretch and you cannot tell by eye when they are distorting the measurement. Keep a sharp pencil and craft knife to hand for marking up the materials and a try-square or combination square to determine right angles. For wall-mounting of shelves or a cupboard, check that the drill is fitted with the right masonry bit and that you have the correct wall plugs and hardware, capable of supporting the structure securely.

Choose materials of the right weight and durability for the type of storage you require – solidly built for long-term use; lightweight for temporary or decorative constructions. Fillers and finishes – paints, stains or varnishes – should be of a type formulated to achieve the best result on the base materials you have chosen. Always check manufacturer's instructions.

## KD fittings

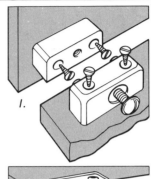

*KD (short for knock-down) fittings offer a quick and easy way to join timber and board.*

*1. Two-part plastic blocks are a little expensive but very neat. Simply screw the halves of the block to the pieces you wish to join, bring together and secure with the machine screw.*

*2. Metal corner plates (usually brass or steel) are more conspicuous, but good for making boxes, chests, etc.*

*3. Metal brackets are best on simple shelving-type structures. L-, T- and X-shaped versions in brass and steel are widely available, and for where extra strength and rigidity are needed, there are also braced designs similar to corner plates.*

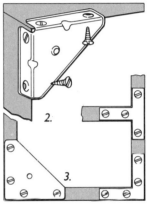

## Making a simple shelf unit

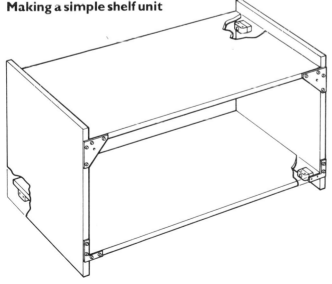

*This shelf unit is the basis of most built-in furniture and converts easily to a box. Mark out and cut the uprights and shelves, ensuring the ends are square, and mark the shelf positions on the side, again checking that they are square.*

*Lay one side piece flat, and fix on the shelves, using KD blocks (see 1. above) under the shelves, and plates and brackets (see 3. above) on the front and back edges. Turn the unit over and repeat the procedure on the second side.*

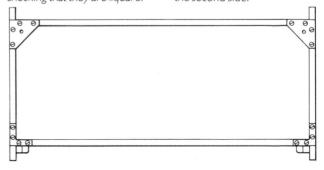

## Wall fixings

*Shelving is only as strong as the wall fixing, so the correct "wall plug" is essential if the screws are to grip.*

*1. Plain plastic anchors are cheapest but need carefully drilled holes leaving the bulk of the anchor embedded in the brickwork – not the wall's plaster coating.*

*2. Ribbed plastic anchors tend to be stronger, particularly in slightly loose material.*

*3. In very soft (concrete or cinderblock) walls, finned cinderblock anchors that you hammer home are best. Cavity walls (stud partitions) present more of a problem.*

*4. & 5. Use a collapsible plastic anchor for plasterboard; a metal toggle both for lath and plaster.*

*For really heavy fixings, screw directly into the wall's timber framework.*

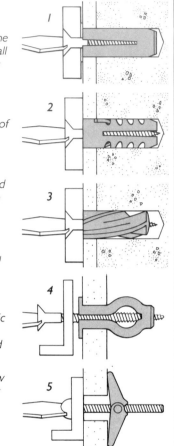

### Wall-mounting – fixings and brackets

Before starting work, check there is no danger of drilling through electric cables or water pipes. Then make sure you have the correct fixing for the type of wall. Exterior walls will be of brick or dense concrete, skimmed over with plaster. For these, and the softer aerated concrete blocks and cinderblock sometimes used in interior walls, use ordinary plastic wall plugs or special cinderblock plugs as appropriate. Stud partitions are also used for internal walls; these consist of a timber framework clad in plasterboard or, in older homes, plaster applied over wooden slats (known as lath and plaster). You can identify stud walls simply by tapping – they sound hollow. For heavy fixings on stud walls, you should screw into the supporting timbers, which you can locate by tapping and test drilling. If they are not in the right place, bridge two or more with a timber batten, and make the final fitting into that. For lighter loads, use special collapsible plastic plugs or metal toggles (better for lath and plaster). Both jam themselves within the wall's cavity, against the inner face of the plaster-work, and so stop the screw pulling out.

Whether you use a hand or electric drill, check that you have a bit of the correct size for the screw or fixing. Mark the place in the wall accurately and start the hole with a bradawl. To ensure you drill to the right depth, mark the measurement with tape on the bit, or use the depth-guide bolt supplied with many drills.

## Screw choices

*1. Countersunk screws – for general woodwork.*
*2. Round head screws – for fixing metal fittings.*
*3. Raised head screws – as above, but countersunk.*
*4. Phillips head screws – easier to drive than slotted types.*
*5. Sheetrock screws – give extra grip in sheetrock.*

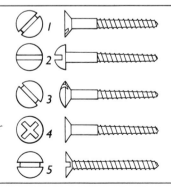

*6. Dome head screws – provide a concealed fixing.*
*7. Screw caps – make screw heads more decorative.*
*8. & 9. Plastic screw covers – push fit or snap-on, hide screw heads.*
*10. Chipboard plugs – let you use ordinary woodscrews instead of sheetrock screws.*

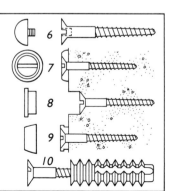

## Shelving

There's a wide range of suitable shelving materials; timber merchants and large do-it-yourself stores offer cut-to-size services and you need only finish visible edges or sand down and paint. Glass makes elegant display shelving but leave cutting to a glazier, who will grind all the edges smooth.

The type of material you choose should depend on the weight it will carry, the strength of supports and distance between them. Good retailers will give you more detailed advice. As a guide, you can assume display shelves need lightweight support; the television, video and rows of hardback books are the heavyweights needing strong support.

## Shelf supports

*Of these basic ways to support shelving, use 1-4 for heavy loads; 5 or 6 for light ones.*

*1. Wall bar and bracket adjustable shelving system.*

*2. Homemade wooden bracket.*

*3. Metal shelf bracket.*

*4. Timber end strips.*

*5. Track and clip adjustable end supports.*

*6. Push-in plastic peg end supports.*

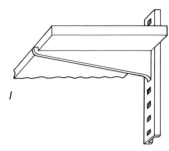

1

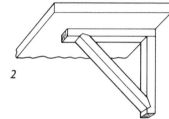

2

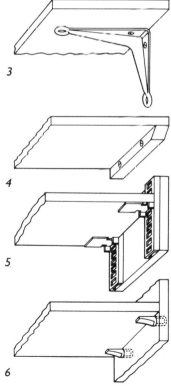

3

4

5

6

## Shelving materials

| MATERIALS | THICKNESSES | COMMENTS |
| --- | --- | --- |
| **Natural timber**<br>Even "cheap" softwood can prove expensive, particularly in shelf widths, which are, in any case, prone to warping. | ½ to 1 inch | For wide shelves from narrower planks glued edge to edge. |
| **Chipboard**<br>Available plain in large sheets, or with hardwood and plastic veneers in a range of useful shelf-sized widths. | ½ to ¾ inch | Edge veneered boards with matching iron-on edging strip or wood edging. |
| **Blockboard**<br>Softwood battens sandwiched between outer veneers; sold mainly in large sheets. | ½ to ¾ inch | Core battens should run the length of the shelf; add wood edging to neaten edges. |
| **Plywood**<br>Thin veneers glued together to prevent warping. Strong but expensive; sold in large sheets. | ½ to 1 inch | Neaten edges with strips of veneer or wood edging. |
| **Medium density fibreboard**<br>Similar to chipboard but stronger. Sold in large sheets. | ½ to 1 inch | Needs only painting to give an attractive finish. |

## Alcove shelving

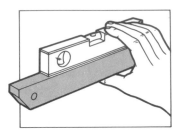

*1. Fix a support horizontally to one side of the alcove.*

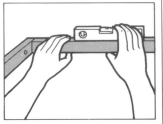

*2. Use it as a guide to positioning the rear support.*

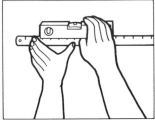

*3. Carry the rear line across to the other side of the alcove.*

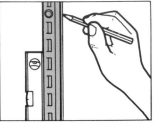

*4. Fix this side support, cut the rear support to fit and secure.*

## Adjustable shelving

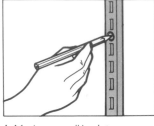

*1. Mark one wall bar's top screw hole and loosely fix in place.*

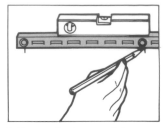

*2. Repeat for the remaining bars, ensuring all bar tops are level.*

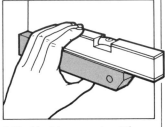

*3. Hold each bar vertically, and mark every other screw hole.*

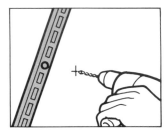

*4. Drill and plug the wall, then screw the wall bars in place.*

### Concealing fittings and lighting

Shelving always looks more professional if the method of fitting is deliberately concealed. If shelves are at eye level or below, brackets are obscured if they protrude no more than two-thirds of the width of the shelf they support. Supports are virtually unseen if the outside edge of the shelf is lipped with a solid strip or molding deeper than the shelf's thickness. Other concealed fittings include wooden dowels or pegs of metal or plastic, which are tapped into pre-drilled holes in wooden uprights at either end of the shelving area. There are also transparent plastic or chromed metal fittings designed to grip glass shelves and prevent them from slipping. It is also possible for shelves to be cantilevered out from a solid wall. This can be very effective, as there are no visible means of support; but as it involves making a recess in the supporting wall and fixing the shelf firmly inside before the final coat of plaster is put on, it needs considerable forethought at planning stage.

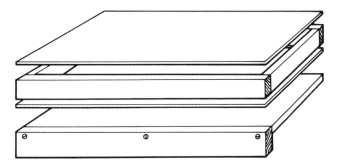

### Concealed fittings

*To conceal the hardware of an alcove shelf, turn the usual supports into a frame and clad with plywood. Elsewhere, merely add a decorative front 'lip'. This can be used to conceal strip lighting if desired.*

## Utility shelf brackets

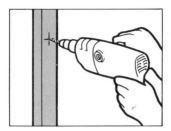

*1.* For garage shelving, fix vertical supports at intervals.

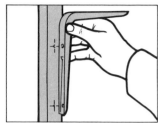

*2.* Mark the bracket fitting holes, so all brackets will be level.

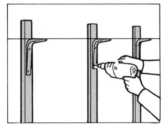

*3.* A screwdriver drill attachment makes fitting the shelves easier.

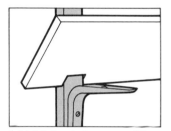

*4.* Notch the shelves around the supports and screw in place.

For convenience, a striplight can be fixed to the inside of an overhanging lip, illuminating the shelf below but concealing the light source. For this sort of detail, shelves and their lighting need to be planned together so that the wiring can be integrated with the early stages of construction. Down-lighters in the ceiling can wash the wall behind shelves fitted with a gap between the back edges and the wall. To avoid rewiring, a couple of uplighters on the floor below the shelving will create a similar effect.

## Hinges

If you are fitting cupboards, or giving old furniture a new look with replacement doors, you need to consider the right type of hinges for the job. Most hinges can be fitted to a door whether it opens on the left- or right-hand side, but some are specifically designed to be fitted on one side or the other.

Surface-mounted and flush hinges have leaves which are fixed directly to a frame and door, whereas butt hinges are

## Useful hinges

There are literally dozens of types of hinge available, covering a range of sizes, styles and materials. However, there are a few you will find particularly useful.

*1.* Surface-mounted hinges are spring-loaded to hold the door securely in the open or closed position.

*2.* Butt hinges are the usual choice for doors fitted flush with cabinet sides.

*3.* Offset hinges let doors open through 180° without obstructing neighboring cabinets.

*4.* Flush hinges, unlike butt hinges, avoid the need to cut rebates in door and frame.

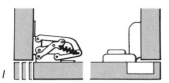

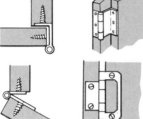

## Making a cupboard

To turn a simple shelf unit into a cupboard, merely add a couple of doors, and perhaps a plywood or masonite back. To increase its versatility, the sides can be drilled to take adjustable shelf supports.

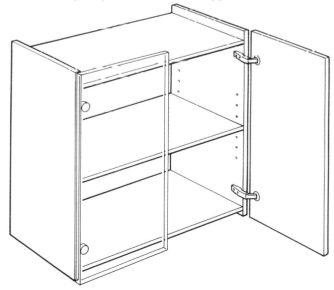

screwed into a recess cut into the side of door and frame. The pivoting section of the hinge, known as the knuckle, projects just beyond the face of the door and frame and the two leaves come together when the door is opened. Kitchen units are commonly fitted with concealed hinges where both parts of the mechanism are hidden within the cabinet. Many of these designs also have an opening angle of 180 degrees. A useful hinge often used on full-overlay doors or self-assembly cupboards is the screw-in pivot. The arms of the hinge are screwed into holes in the sides of door and frame, so only the neat bolt of the pivot hinge is visible. Doors fitted in this way can be lifted off for easy cleaning or painting.

## Finishing

Old furniture can be dramatically improved if stripped of the layers of paint or varnish accumulated over the years, which disguise the natural warm quality of the original material and often conceal interesting features and moldings. Of course, some furniture was made to be painted and the wood can look unattractive if stripped bare, when knots and irregular grain patterns may be revealed.

Varnish is best removed with a chemical stripper. Large articles can be painted with a paste or blanket stripper, but this method requires further washing with water and is unsuitable for veneered pieces. Hot-air strippers, the modern and safer equivalent of the blow torch, are very effective for removing paint but care is needed as scorch marks are difficult to remedy. When removing old paint, never dig at stubborn areas with a metal scraper. Apply more stripper and use steel wool to rub along the grain. Small cracks and holes may be stopped with commercial fillers which can be colored to match the wood. It's easiest to overfill the hole and sand off the excess when the filler is dry.

Stripped wood can be finished with a hardwearing polyurethane varnish or sealed with a wax or oil finish; the latter are more traditional but neither heat-resistant nor waterproof. The color of the wood itself can be lightened by special bleach treatment or darkened with wood stain in a natural shade or one of the various colors available.

### Iron-on edging

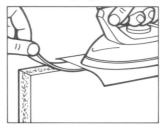 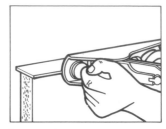

*Position the edging strip so it overlaps both faces of the chipboard and, protecting its surface with paper, smooth it into place with a warm iron.*

*Remove the excess with a smoothing plane set for a very fine cut, angling this to give a slight chamfer. Give a final smoothing using sandpaper.*

### Edging with wood

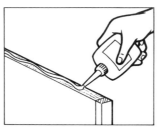 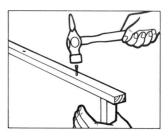

*Where no great strength is required, wood edging can merely be glued on. If possible, cramp tightly in place while the glue sets.*

*Reinforce the glue with push pins. Punch the heads below the surface and cover with putty.*

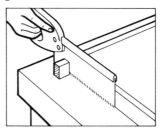 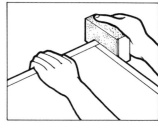

*For neatness, use side pieces that are too long, and remove the excess with a saw and plane, once all the edging has been firmly glued in place.*

*Finish off by sanding, paying particular attention to the corners and any endgrain.*

## Stripping the surface

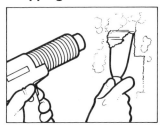

A modern hot-air electric paint stripper is best on large areas. Soften the existing paint, then scrape off using a broad-bladed, flat scraper.

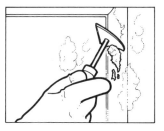

To scrape the softened paint out of awkward corners and moldings, use a shavehook – the combination type shown is the most versatile.

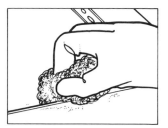

Liquid chemical strippers let you scrub out complex moldings using steel wool. Wear thick rubber gloves, and follow the safety instructions on the can.

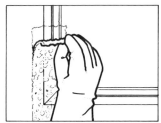

Peel-off, blanket-type chemical strippers are an easier, though only slightly less messy, alternative. However, they are expensive over large areas.

## Filling

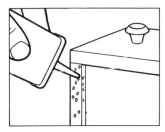

Treat woodworm-affected timber with a commercial insecticide/preservative.

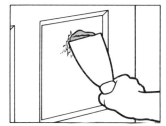

Fill cracks and holes using wood filler or, if you intend to varnish, wood putty.

## Sanding down

Use a powered orbital sander to smooth large, flat areas ready for the final decorative finish.

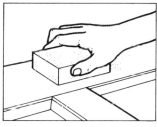

Sandpaper wrapped round a cork block is better for sanding small, awkward areas.

## Applying the finish

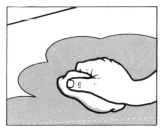

Stains and thin primer coats of polyurethane can be rubbed in using a soft, lint-free cloth.

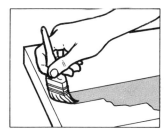

Paint and top coats of varnish should be brushed on in a series of thin, even coats.

## Stenciling

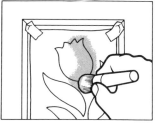

Ready-cut stencils are now easily available. "Stab" paint through using a bristly stencil brush.

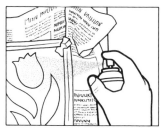

Stencils can also be spray painted, after masking the surrounding area with newspaper.

# INDEX

kitchen units (contd)
  in workrooms 64
kitchens, breakfast bar in *37*
  color in *36*
  cooking zone 33, *33*
  fitted 21
  layouts *30*
  multi-purpose 62
  for one-room living 24, 26, 28
  peninsular units 40
  planning 28, 37
  preparation zone 34-35, *34-35*, *36*, 37
  safety points 29
  shelving *31*
  storing for convenience 11
  unit sizes 37
  utensil storage 30, *31*, *32*, 34
  wall treatment *31*
  washing zone 30, 33
  worktops 19, 34
knife racks 34-35, *35*
  in workshops 64
knock-down fittings 71, *71*

ladders, pulley systems for 64
landings 66-67
laundry, with sewing area 62
lighting 6, *6-7*, 22, 54
  concealed 45, 74, *74*
  for display 9
living/dining rooms 38
living rooms *8-9*, 15, 16, *22-23*, 42-45, 60

mantelpieces 9, 44
media storage 11, 45, 62
  concealing 44-45
  customized 18
  modular 12
  on trolleys 19
medicine cupboards 54
meters, concealing 66
mirrors, in bathrooms 54, *54*
  on doors 49
  in kitchens *31*
  on wardrobes *10*, *24-25*, 66
modular storage 12, *12-13*
  as added insulation 44
  bedside chest 12
  doors on 12
  for one-room living 26

movable storage 19, *19*

open-plan system *22-23*
one-room living 24-27, 28
ottoman 45
oven gloves 11, 33
ovens/hobs 33, *33*

paint, removing 76, 77
pantry 22, 33, 34
pegboards, in utility rooms 63
  in workshops 64, *65*, 68, *70*
plant holders 12, 55
platforms, *6-7*
  in bedrooms 46
  in children's rooms 58
  in halls 66
  for one-room living *24-25*, 26-27
  wall-to-wall 66
playrooms 20, *22-23*, 63

racks, on cupboard doors 35
  magnetic 34
radiators, in bathrooms 52
  concealed 16, *42-43*
refrigerators 34
rods, for kitchen utensils 34
room dividers *19*
  from freestanding units 38
  modular 12
  for one-room living 26, *26-27*
  from shelving 38
  under stairs 67

safety, in bathrooms 53, 54-55
  in kitchens 29
seating, over storage 22, 41, *42-43*, 67
self-assembly units 13, 18, *19*
sewing centres/rooms 20, 60, 62, 63
sewing machines 40
shelving 21, 22, 68, *69*, *73*
  adjustable 26, 34, *57*, 58, 62, *74*
  in alcoves 44, *44*, *46-47*, 70, *74*, *74*
  in basements 64
  in bathrooms 52-53, 54
  in bedrooms 46, *46-47*
  for books 12, *42-43*, 67
  brackets for *75*

shelving (contd)
  in children's rooms 56-57, 58
  for china/glass 33, 40, *40*
  chopping blocks 34
  on coffee tables 45
  concealed fixings for 74, *74*
  bedside cupboards 70
  custom-built 16
  doors on 44
  drawers under 55
  as dressing table 51
  end of unit *33*
  finishing 68
  floor-to-ceiling 66
  glass 45, 55, 67, *68*
  in halls 66
  in home offices 62
  industrial 64
  kitchen *31*, 35, 37
  in larders 34
  lighting 22
  in living rooms *42-43*, 44
  making simple unit *71*
  materials 73
  modular 12, *13*
  for one-room living 26-27, 27
  open *9*, 37
  planning 70
  for plants 64
  over radiators 42, 66
  as room-dividers 38
  on runners 44
  as seats 56
  self-assembly 18
  as serving counters 41
  as sleeping platforms 56
  supports for *73*
  in utility rooms 63, *75*
  wall of 22
  across windows 67
  around windows *68*
  in workshops 64
  as writing desk 51
shoe racks 49
shower cubicle 20
sideboards 41
  on shelving *69*
  under stairs 66-67
side-tables, mobile 19
sofa, for one-room living 27
speakers, positioning 45
spice racks 34

staircases *22-23*, 63, 66, *66-67*
studio, in attic 63
studio apartments, kitchen in 28

tables, collapsible 38
  in halls 66
  modular 12
  for one-room living 27
tie/scarf racks 51
towel rails, as drawer handles *55*
  home-made 52
  telescopic 33
'tower' units, for children 58
trays, stacking, in bathrooms 26
trolleys 15, 19, 41
  in bathrooms 55
  in children's rooms 58
typewriters 40

utility rooms 63, *65*
utensils 30, *31*, *32*, 34

vacuum cleaner 11

wall fixings 72, *72*
wallhangings (canvas), for children's clothes 58
washing machines 33, 52
waste bins, in bathrooms 55
  in kitchens 30
  as modular storage *13*
  as plant holders 55
wardrobes 51
  box rooms as 20
  built-in 49, *50*, 66
  clothes rails as 48
  concealed *49*
  customizing 21
  drawers in 22
  floor-to-ceiling 49
  under bed 46
  mirrored *10*, *24-25*, 66
  in nursery 58
  for one-room living *27*
  in walk-in cupboards *51*
windows, storage around *68*
windowseats 67
wine racks 41
  in fireplaces *68*
  as shoe racks 49
  under stairs *66-67*

# Acknowledgments

The author would like to thank Sidney Langford

Illustrations by Hayward & Martin

Picture credits:
Abbreviations: CO – Conran Octopus Ltd; EWA – Elizabeth Whiting & Associates; *MMC – La Maison de Marie Claire; WOI – The World of Interiors*

*Abitare*/Silvio Wolf 49, Claudio Santini 61; Camera Press 22-3, 24-5, 25, 26-7, 31 right, 38-9, 42-3, 54, 55, 62-3, 64, 68 below right; Gilles de Chabaneix 6-7, 21 left; *House & Garden*/Arabella McNair Wilson 32; CO/Simon Brown 34-5 (architect: Shay Cleary), 46-7, 66-7; EWA 10; EWA/John Bouchier 11; EWA/Michael Dunne 51; EWA/Michael Nicholson 69; EWA/Julian Nieman 14 right; EWA/Spike Powell 56, 57, 68 above right; EWA/Tim Street-Porter 67; EWA/Friedhelm Thomas 16-17; EWA/Jerry Tubby 69 below left; *Good Housekeeping*/Jan Baldwin 15, 28-9, 31 left; Habitat 12-13, 19 (all), 36, 41, 48; Interlübke Ltd 27; Ken Kirkwood 21 right, 40, 59 right, 69 above; *MMC*/Yves Duronsoy 9; *MMC*/Pierre Hussenot 14, 68 left; *MMC*/Serge Korniloff 37; *MMC*/Claude Pataut 8-9, 33 (both); Bill McLaughlin 17, 45; Octopus Books Ltd 65; Poggenpohl 35 (both); Jessica Strang 59 left, 70; *Sunday Express Magazine*/Simon Brown 52-3; Syndication International 44; *WOI*/Michael Boys 50; *WOI*/Richard Bryant 60-1